SHAKE
THE
ANGER
HABIT!

Betty Doty • Pat Rooney

The Bookery Publishing Company - 8193 Riata Dr., Redding, CA 96002

—Books by Betty Doty & Pat Rooney

THE ANGER PUZZLE
SHAKE THE ANGER HABIT!

—Books by Betty Doty

BREAK THE ANGER TRAP
MARRIAGE INSURANCE
PUBLISH YOUR OWN HANDBOUND BOOKS

—Audio Cassettes

SHAKE THE ANGER HABIT! (the essentials)
SHAKE THE ANGER HABIT! (entire book)

Library of Congress Cataloging-in-Publication Data

Doty, Betty.
    Shake the anger habit! / Betty Doty, Pat Rooney. -- Rev. ed.
        p.   cm.
    Includes bibliographical references and index.
    ISBN 0-930822-10-2 (pbk. : alk. paper) : $11.95
    1. Anger.   I. Rooney, Pat, 1926-   II. Title.
BJ1535.A6D68   1990
152.4'7--dc20   90-43496
                                                      CIP

First printing 1987
Second printing 1988
Third printing 1990 (revised edition)

Table of Contents

TABLE OF CONTENTS
(Continued)

Foreword

*I first read Betty Doty and Pat Rooney's approach to anger because I wanted to be aware of as many treatment resources for my patients as possible, but I found that their analysis and channeling of anger was helping me with my own relationships — even my marriage was better! Since at least three-fourths of the stresses my patients experience involve anger to some extent, I often "prescribe" **Shake the Anger Habit**. In fact, I keep a box of "Shakes" in my office all the time.*

It gives me great pleasure to recommend this book, whether from my office or from this foreword.

R. Guilford Fitz, M.D.
Family Practice, Redding, California
Asst. Clinical Professor of Family Practice
    on faculty at University of California
    at Davis, California

The newest part of this revised edition of **SHAKE THE ANGER HABIT!** is "The Angry Pleasers," page 173.

I'm eternally grateful to everyone who has contributed to the writing of this book. Especially valuable has been Pat Rooney's information and encouragement as well as his help with seminars, workshops and talkshows. Thank you!

— Betty Doty

Chapter 1

Shaking the anger habit

Does your anger embarrass you? isolate you? push others away when you want them close?

If so, you too can learn to shake the anger habit.

Will it be easy and painless? Maybe, as just recognizing anger as a habit opens up new possibilities. You can substitute a new habit without too much difficulty, once your **thinking** about anger changes. And it's true that the new habit can be developed from reading this one book.

But isn't anger a feeling? One that comes too fast for thought? Of course it seems that way, especially after a lifetime of rushing through the same thought patterns. But our feelings don't just come out of nowhere. Instead they come from the habitual way we're processing information. With a longstanding habit of telling ourselves we ought to be angry about certain things, we don't need to be reconvinced each time. The trigger works easily...too easily for our own and others' comfort.

To break the mindset which activates anger, we simply use our mind to re-examine old thinking habits. That's why just reading this book can make a difference in the way each reader learns to process *all* information.

"Now wait a minute," you might be saying. "It will affect the way I process *all* information? Maybe you're going to tell me to avoid anger just by wearing rose-colored glasses?"

Definitely not, and I won't be recommending wearing dark glasses either. What I'll be suggesting is the exact opposite: forming the habit of learning to see the world *more and more clearly*. If we wear any glasses at all, they will seem to be *cleaner* than ever.

It won't be too difficult to form the habit of sharpening our observations (putting on the cleaner glasses), when we realize the tremendous changes...for the better...which can occur.

Surely you don't think it's possible to learn to erase the anger habit totally? You're right, I don't expect that. But from reading this book, at least one thing will be clear: After each incidence of anger, you'll be able to see exactly how it works against you, how it drives others away...in the long run. And after learning **how** to shake the anger habit, you won't be choosing anger again and again (unless you really **enjoy** being alone...isolated.)

Isn't anger ever justified? Does it make any difference if we believe anger is justified if it doesn't work for us? if it doesn't get us what we want in the long run? (We can always be like the drivers who are bent on proving they are right, dead right.)

So why do any of us use anger (criticism, blaming or other forms of anger) when eventually it brings isolation? As far as I can tell, we repeat the anger habit simply because we haven't found a better alternative. We haven't learned, yet, to form another habit **which gives better results.**

In this book you'll find specific suggestions for escaping the personal trap we create by our own anger. You'll probably very much enjoy finding a route which leads to better long-range feelings for yourself...and for those around you.   □

Chapter 2

Finding an alternative

Why is it that so much anger abounds, maybe to epidemic proportions, yet we have so much trouble finding an alternative?

I've come to believe that many of us, if not most, have gone along with a **wrong turn** in our overall thinking about anger. It's as if the standard information we've been repeatedly passing around to each other (the so-called conventional wisdom), not only has failed to bring anger levels down, but it is actually perpetuating and increasing anger.

What is this conventional wisdom that "everybody knows" about anger? Let's look closely at three of the most common beliefs.

The ***first*** is that "everybody knows" it's bad to hold anger inside. It might come out too fast, at the wrong time and place...and cause terrible embarrassment, or worse.

A **second** "everybody knows" is that since it's bad to hold anger inside, it **must** be better to get it out.

And a **third** "everybody knows" is hastily added to the second, "but of course we ought to get the anger out safely."

You're probably wondering why I say this collection of what "everybody knows" actually increases and perpetuates anger. You may want to look back over the three beliefs and see if you can guess.

Maybe you've noticed the **total** focus of what "everybody knows" is on **how** we get anger out, as if that is **all that matters**. ("Don't bury it, just get it out...safely, of course.")

It seems evident that our society's near obsession with getting anger out has blocked a view of the opposite end of the scale, **the way we form anger in the first place.**

It's as if we took one look at full-blown rage and figured all we could do was get out of the way. It became an "everybody knows" that anger is inevitable, and it just didn't occur to us to look backward, carefully enough, to examine the way anger is formed.

Of course, it's been necessary to give a high priority to dealing with the effects of anger, both personally and as a society. But when we **continue** to avert our eyes from the cause of anger and **continue** to believe that **all** that matters is how we get it out after it's formed, the more deeply rooted and dangerous the anger epidemic becomes.

It appears to me that our society as a whole has entered a trap formed by our myths about anger. And from that position it's been nearly impossible to get far enough outside the trap to be able to find alternatives to forming anger.   □

Chapter 3

Looking at beliefs about anger

Let's look for a minute at what happens in a society which holds to the belief that "good guys" get anger out and only "bad guys" hold it in. Just look around you and keep your eyes open. What do you see?

What I see is that **too often too many of us are afraid of each other's anger.**

Criticism, blaming and judgmentalness abound, constantly triggering fears of such criticism, blaming and judgmentalness.

> "Look at her. She must have gained twenty pounds. Pretty soon she'll be called the girl with no neck."

When I hear teenagers talk, I wonder that any of them have the courage to leave their homes for school each morning.

One result of so much fear of each other's anger is that people seem to be increasingly afraid of making decisions. Maybe we choose to work with endless committees and consultants, just following any leader, maybe, in order to "pass the buck."

Our desperate need to find safety from blaming, judgmentalness and criticism may be the first priority in our lives. This can result in a withdrawing to personal depression, and I suspect that such depression may be the number one health problem in our country today. It's as if many people are trying harder and harder to be free of criticism and enjoying their lives less and less.

I think of Alvin Toffler's book **FUTURE SHOCK** and his theme that the rate of change has become so great that many people are becoming overwhelmed, nearly paralyzed and unable to adapt to more changes.

This makes me think that maybe our anger at each other has reached such a dangerous point that *too* many of us, *too* much of the time, are *too* afraid of others' anger. And our most elementary functioning is becoming increasingly more difficult.

Yet I see anger spreading like wildfire. If we could add the total quantity of society's self-anger (usually called guilt) to the total quantity of anger directed at people, situations or inanimate objects, we'd see that our collective anger level is tremendously high.

How much more anger can a society tolerate?

When **too** many of us are retreating to safety from criticism, it means that **too** many of us feel the need to blame others in order to divert pressure from ourselves.

But look at the problem we've created for **ourselves**. Not only have we made those we blamed uncomfortable (if not a danger to us), but our blame-placing has a more serious unwanted side-effect **for ourselves**. In order to stay blameless, **we have to see ourselves as helpless:** "It's all their fault ... I can't do anything..." We ourselves are forced to assume a helpless position: *"Isn't it obvious I can't do anything?"*

But helplessness is an **enormous price to pay** for what we believe is safety for ourselves. And this is especially true when we realize that helplessness itself often triggers **our own anger**, which creates the **opposite** of any real safety.

At a barbecue recently someone complained about the pickles, "They're too squishy." Someone else said, "Bad Joe," as

Joe had chosen the pickles at the store. Another said, "Bad store," and another came in with "Bad food processing company...they used the wrong recipe."

As we were laughing, an interesting truth became apparent. How many times does it happen, when people are talking together, that someone starts a conversation by mentioning a problem. Then the talk goes on **just long enough** for the group to agree on who or what to blame, and the discussion ends. It's as if the problem has been laid to rest.

"... It's those politicians ... the CIA ... the Commies ... the military-industrial complex ... cheap labor abroad ... labor union leaders ... greedy capitalists ... environmentalists ... permissiveness ... me-first generation ... the Rockefellers ... the profit motive ... the Japanese ... the courts ... attorneys ... schools ... TV ... the media ... parents ... working women ... women's lib ... absent fathers ... teenagers ... the neighbors ... shoddy workmanship ... Madison Avenue ... Wall Street ... the system ... my ex-wife/husband ... mother-in-law ... the devil made me do it..." (Have I missed any?)

What price do we pay for such conclusions except our own helplessness?

Isn't it likely that at the root of our seemingly separate problems is one primary problem, the one created by the myth that we need to get our anger out? the myth which keeps us living in fear of each other's anger? Isn't it possible that we'll stay within this pattern (going from fear of anger to trying to find safety, to finding, instead, helplessness and anger) until we look more closely at anger itself and the way it is formed?

Actually I see the need to re-examine our beliefs about anger as being forced upon us.

- How many more stress reduction classes can be scheduled?

- Can we ever build enough courtrooms and jails?

- Who pays for the job burnout stemming from anger? (the employer? insurance companies? all of us?)

What about economic productivity? Is the widespread need for buck-passing, and the resulting depression and apathy, taking a crucial toll in this area? Is the need for countless committees and consultants (because individuals fear making decisions) limiting our productivity?

In my own profession, I see among my colleagues the result of what appears to be the need to seek safety from anger. (Who wouldn't sometimes want to find a way to escape the firing line, *in any profession*, in a society of so much blame-placing and litigation?) Many of my fellow professionals do a certain kind of research which means sending out innumerable questionnaires. Of course the purpose is to get information, but by getting it exclusively *from others*, it is a method which keeps the researchers safe from criticism.

But I can see adverse results for the rest of us (based on the findings of surveys I see in my own profession).

Have you *ever* filled in one questionnaire which elicited information which accurately portrayed your views? Or did the questions, composed from another's point of view, somehow hit you wrong?

Is it *any* surprise that the results of such surveys often don't *quite* ring true? Yet such results form the basis for more and more research in the field of human relations which also may not *quite* ring true? (Maybe this compares to a surveyor's being off only one foot for the first mile...)

I cannot escape the conclusion that we are paying a tremendously high price for the scramble for safety which results from our fear of each other's anger (the fear that arises when "everybody knows" that we need to get our anger out). ☐

Chapter 4

Managing anger: a myth

Let's look at the three most common ways of handling anger, all based on the assumption that it's good to get it out. I believe each method pushes others away in the long run as others feel unsafe with us.

The **first** method recommended for getting anger out is to "talk it out" with a third party. **And sometimes this may work.** But how many people do you know who have been angry as long as you've known them, and are also continually expressing their anger? Is there any real evidence that expressing anger dissipates it? or does it actually magnify it and attract allies?

The **second method**, much approved for getting anger out harmlessly, is with physical exercise, maybe just hitting a punching bag or pillow or running or bike-riding. Does this work? Yes, if our only goal is releasing physical tension. But I can't see that exercise does anything to help us break the **habit** of forming anger again and again ... and pushing others away ... again and again.

A **third** way to get anger out comes from the idea that we ought to learn to "stand up on our own two feet" (to use the most common cliché) and tell the target of our anger why we're mad (or hurt).

Let's look at some of the reasons this method really doesn't get us what we want (except for temporary release of tension).

First, there's a problem for people who hold their anger as long as they can and then see it all burst out (unbidden) at the tiniest provocation.

I used to believe that in order to avoid the disaster of such a gigantic blowup, it would help to become more aware of our anger building up. Then we could choose to let it out oftener, in smaller quantities, at the right target and at the right time and place. That seemed so logical.

But I now believe that it's impossible to be able to talk to the target of our anger about our hurt and anger...in ways which work for us and our targets in the long run.

If our habit is to bury anger, we do it for one good reason: **extreme fear of our own**

anger. It's a fear borne of experience that losing control means untold negative effects, not only on others, but for ourselves, as it reinforces our own "bad guy" feelings. (***"Could I possibly have done** that?"*)

We would rather keep ourselves up-tight, unfeeling and barely able to enjoy life, rather than risk the effects of trying to talk about our anger to the target of our anger. To us it not only ***seems*** impossible, but it probably ***is*** impossible to learn to calmly say, "I get mad when you do that..." The fear is simply too overwhelming that one wrong word might lead to an uncontrollable explosion.

Let's look now at those of us who have no trouble telling the targets of our anger why we're hurt and angry. In fact, we stay in good practice. Does such telling help or hinder?

By putting ourselves in the position of being the target of another's hurt and anger, we can easily see that critics usually get the opposite of what they want.

Let's examine the most common ways of responding to criticism (and judging, blaming and all other forms of anger and non-acceptance) directed at us.

Criticism often is perceived as an attempt to control us. And it doesn't really matter what the tone of voice, or how carefully the criticism is given. The basic message we believe we are hearing from the other is this: "Because I hurt (or am angry) and don't approve of what you're doing, you really shouldn't be doing it."

Let's look at the three most common responses to this message.

When criticism comes, response **number one** may be to feel guilty, defensive and somewhat confused: "Yeah, she's right, I'm a rat... but I try to do what she wants and it just doesn't feel right..." The inevitable result is that rather than stay around and continually be the target of such anger, we remove ourselves from the critic whenever possible.

Number two response (if we're on the receiving end of criticism) may be instant resistance. Just because the other pushes in one direction, we repeatedly do the opposite. This means we stay locked up in a series of power struggles.

Let's take a quick look to see why power struggles can't work for us in the long run.

You probably know what it's like when a person feels the need to be one-up all the time. It means living in fear that another will get the upper hand ... or has already gotten it.

We'll say two boys are throwing rocks, starting first with small pebbles and increasing in size. Then they bring in older brothers, and maybe into adulthood, attorneys and armies.

But the problem stays the same, no matter what the size of the power struggle or the details. Winning by force can't really feel good, as there is always the knowledge that the losers are only too eager to spoil the winnings.

Such a power-struggle lifestyle (of continually feeling either one-up or one-down) blocks learning to relate to each other as equals. It stays impossible to learn how to get the best out of others. Because we continually get the worst out of those around us, we repeatedly conclude that it's necessary to fight harder and harder.

This means that more and more futile rounds of power struggles are begun, as we don't know how to stop the merry-go-round.

Response **number three** (when we're the target of another's criticism) is just as certain to push us away, although it doesn't seem so at first.

This response is made when we don't want to be like the bad guys we see around us (those who do ridiculous things out of guilt and rebelliousness).

As the recipient of another's anger, we choose, instead, to be "good guys." When the critic says, in essence, "I feel bad so you should be different so I can feel better," the "good guy" would say, "Yes, you're right...I should have done this instead of that...I'll try even harder than ever to do what you want."

In the next two chapters we'll look at some of the reasons why trying to please others plays such a big part in the way we form anger...and the way we learn to shake the anger habit.   □

Chapter 5

Fearing anger, our own and others'

A husband and wife are fighting, and the husband tells the wife she isn't the way he wants her to be. She doesn't want him to be angry and unhappy so she panics and says, "I'll change...just tell me what I need to do." So she tries to change, but inevitably returns to her usual behavior. So the husband throws a fit again (or maybe just withdraws), she panics again, and she tries to change again...and the cycle repeats...again.

Both continue to define the problem in ways which keep themselves helpless in making things better. (And if this isn't clear yet, it probably will be by the time you finish reading this book.)

> Wife: "I ought to be able to please him."
>
> Husband: "If she'd just do what she ought to do I'd accept her and treat her better."

For some couples this becomes a perpetual roller coaster, with maybe ups and downs coming at shorter intervals, continuing because both achieve at least temporary pay-offs. (The husband gets reassurance from his wife's attempts to change, as he believes those are signs she cares for him. The wife interprets his treating her better, even for a short time, as evidence of true caring.)

The longer they feel the discomfort of the roller coaster lifestyle, the more they need reassurance that the other cares. Even short-term reassurance seems better than none, and if the roller coaster is the only way they know how to get it, they stay on it.

You can easily imagine the complexity of a situation in which **both** people are unaccepting of each other, and **both** believe the other ought to change in order to make things better, and **both** are trying to please the other in order to avoid the other's anger and non-acceptance.

I can flatly say, from my experience inside and outside the counseling room, that *relating to another person by constantly*

trying to please means we stay headed down a dead-end street.

To show how far this desire to please can go (even though the efforts to please consistently foster isolation instead of closeness), I'll tell you what a husband told me in the counseling room: He said that his wife had asked his permission to kill herself.

Because the wife was so compulsive in her attempt to please others (hence her despair and nearness to suicide at that time), she couldn't bear the thought of her husband's being displeased with her ***even after her death.*** □

Chapter 6

Knowing we can't avoid anger

When we're responding to anger and criticism by trying to please others, what really is wrong with that? If we're unhappy ourselves, isn't it all right to ease our own pain a little by pleasing others...at least occasionally?

Let's look at a compulsive pleaser.

A woman was tired of failing to please her husband, so she decided to ask him to write out, in much detail, exactly what he wanted for breakfast in bed. His note began, "I want two eggs, one boiled and one fried, three slices of bacon, cooked flat, not all curled up..."

The woman took great pains to be certain she complied with each detail of the instructions, even adding a fresh rose to the corner of the breakfast tray.

The husband took one look and said, "You fried the wrong egg."

Some readers may think, "What a bad husband, impossible to please..." But notice the real source of the woman's pain: *She evidently believed she had the power to please her husband...and get appreciation...if only she'd try hard enough.*

Probably each time she failed to get the expected appreciation, her first reaction may have been to feel justified in being angry with her husband. After all, it seemed so obvious, from her point of view, that he was the villain: *He refused to be pleased so he was blocking her from feeling that she's a good wife.*

But a second thought probably was this, "I've got to try harder. I'd be worthless if I couldn't do something as simple as pleasing my husband."

Yet it is apparent to me that the woman had only failed at doing an impossible job...pleasing any other person except herself.

Such pleasing is clearly impossible because only we ourselves decide if we're pleased or not. *We alone control that button*.

It's true that we can get temporary pleasure when someone does something we like. That's because we usually interpret such acts as evidence of others' caring. But then there are the hours and minutes when we are alone with ourselves, and we can only be happy by whatever is inside us.

It's learning to cultivate this thing, discover this button, which enables us to feel happy. As far as I can tell, this is our foremost personal priority. (And getting our anger level down is part of this process.)

I see no alternative to discovering that we ourselves have the power to feel good about ourselves, no matter what the situation. When we develop that capacity, we can take it with us wherever we go.

Otherwise we stay stuck, continually looking for our happiness out there somewhere. We **constantly** criticize whatever it is that we find and stay disappointed. *That's because whatever we find, it can't do what we think it ought to be able to do ... make us happy inside.*

When our reaction to disappointment is anger (because the world and the people in it aren't made the way we think they ought to be), others feel our lack of acceptance and withdraw. Because of our lack of acceptance of others, it becomes more and more difficult to get any kind of cooperation from those who are now out of reach. Whatever our goals, they have become more distant than ever, so we are disappointed more often and we react in anger more often.

A typical way of thinking (and talking) reveals this pattern: *"If only* I had this I'd be happy... *if only* I had that..."* It's apparent that those who talk this way believe that they will find happiness somewhere, out there, if they'll just try hard enough.

The futility of trying to please another (and maybe *devoting our life to it* as a route to expected happiness), is seen when we realize that we become totally in another person's control. It's as if we are doomed to be continually trying this, then trying that, even though we know we are **constantly** ending up in blind alleys. By the time this pattern is totally entrenched, we are truly desperate. We feel blocked at finding happiness, yet helpless to find a better way of relating.

Earlier I wrote about the consequences in a society in which we live in fear of each other's anger, as "everybody knows" we really ought to be getting our anger out. I've mentioned that one of the consequences is that we are afraid to make decisions because of our need to seek safety from criticism.

Trying to please another person, which means taking cues for our own behavior from another, is just one of many ways of seeking safety. Our attempt to avoid anger keeps us helpless. But the resulting helplessness and blame-placing keeps circling back to helplessness and anger... no real safety.

I had one client, near suicide when he came in, who was married, had children and a job. But he told me that he could never be with more than one person at a time. When he was with just one person, he could take on the coloration of that person. But when one more person entered the area, he had to withdraw, as he felt he couldn't please two people at once. Yet he felt worthless if he wasn't pleasing someone.

It is no wonder that he was near suicide, as he didn't know an alternative way of living.

Part of the problem, if we're pleasers, is that we too often use our own frame of reference to figure out what we ought to be doing to please. Of course, such mind-reading is impossible. Even when others try to tell us what they want, they truly don't know. Maybe they are thinking, "I'm unhappy, and I **think** if you'd do this or that I'd be happier." Since the person is just guessing, if we respond by trying to fill the other's requests, we may end up like a puppet dancing on a string (maybe **actually believing** we should have fried the other egg).

Every day in the counseling room I see people who are angry because they aren't able to get the appreciation they believe they deserve (for being so good and "pleasing" others). You'll be reading more and more about this, as martyrs really don't feel good when they neglect their own needs and persist in believing that they **can** know what another wants...and deliver it...**and still feel good about themselves.**

Often two people stay angry because they continually are disappointed that they can't get expected appreciation from a partner. Both tend to believe that the problem is the bad partner who won't give them what they need. So both continue to be angry and draw apart, maybe believing they should look for better partners...ones who can make them happy, as they believe good partners ought to be able to do.

I particularly see this tragic pattern in the counseling room with people who have been married several times. They usually vow to work harder **this time**. And that usually means they plan to try even harder...to please.

Before leaving the subject of trying to please, I want to note that things come out best, from my point of view, when we make choices about what we do for **our own reasons**. That keeps us from getting angry at others for not giving us appreciation. Instead it's as if each transaction is complete. We do what we do and feel good about our choice. Any pat on the head from another would be a bonus, not a necessity.

Of course this doesn't mean that we won't be complying with another's wishes occasionally. But overall, I'll be writing more and more about keeping our own balance, and that means feeling good about ourselves so we're enjoying our own choices...made for our own reasons. ☐

Chapter 7

Making accurate observations

Each small step in the process of learning to shake the anger habit rests on the step before. Maybe sometimes you've felt I've left you hanging, as if I'd dropped the ball too soon. But my plan is to work all the loose ends together before we're through.

I'll jump ahead now to tell you the way the anger habit is broken. It's done by substituting another habit, the habit of making better and better observations.

To show how easy this is going to be, let me explain a little more. When I write about making better observations (as if our glasses have become cleaner), it means reminding ourselves **constantly** of the need to keep checking our observations and making predictions. By comparing results of the predictions with what we expected, and rechecking our observations, we can make more predictions...which are a check on the accuracy of our original observations.

When we look at a wide view of anger which includes the way it is formed, a different picture comes into focus. We find we really don't have to build our lifestyle based on scaring each other with our anger (or even minor disapproval) after all. And we don't really have to spend our lives frantically trying to find safety from others' anger.

By the time you finish reading I believe you too will see that forming anger isn't inevitable at all, and getting anger out (after it's formed) also isn't inevitable.

When Pat Rooney and I do seminars and workshops, we get tremendous feedback for what we do in three hours. So we know that perfectly ordinary people can learn to shake the anger habit in a fairly short time. In order for you to reinforce some of the basics before you read on, here is a brief review.

1) If anger doesn't work in our favor in the long run, why do we use it? (page 5)

2) What is the point of the story which ends with the line, "You fried the wrong egg?" (page 30)

3) I suggested three reasons it doesn't work for us when we tell the target of our hurt and anger about our hurt and anger. Do you remember all three reasons? (page 22)

4) How does fear of making decisions become a by-product of what "everybody knows" about anger? (page 11)

□

NOT GETTING THROUGH

ANGER

Chapter 8

Trying to understand each other

When I write about getting through to others, I mean it in the sense that we feel really heard and deeply understood, if possible.

As you can see by the diagram, not getting through leads to anger. But anger leads back to not getting through (as others will be pulling away from us).

Yet if we become desperate enough to get through, we'll discover that **enough** anger will **always** guarantee a kind of getting through, an ugly kind, a kind with unwanted repercussions. But our desperateness may repeatedly push us to use anger as a certain short-cut to getting through: it's like finding a knife for the heart, a weapon we can always have with us.

Probably all of us know how important it is to feel we can get through to others, and we know how desperate and panicky we feel when we can't. Maybe we feel helpless, dead-ended, as if we're hitting a stone wall.

For couples who come into the counseling room, as far as I can tell, the reason they are here is that they feel they can't get through to each other...*without anger.* Even though each knows that anger pushes the other away, they truly may not have been able to cultivate getting-through skills without anger. So they **continually** need anger, the knife to the heart, as a certain method of getting through.

The result is that both feel **continually** pushed away, and they both **continually** blame the other, and both are in no position to be learning long-range getting-through skills. There never seems to be a **good time** to learn a more effective alternative.

After all, maybe it seems better to be an angry "bad guy" than a nobody? one who can't even get through at all? one who can't have any real impact?

NOT GETTING THROUGH

ANGER

Something sad occurs with many people who want to be "good guys" and conclude it's best to keep their feelings out of sight. Probably they've found that the **only time** they can say how they feel (if it's critical) may be when propelled by **enough** anger. **Then the erroneous conclusion is reached that they always lose when they tell another person how they feel.** Of course it is the anger which makes the situation worse instead of better. But the need for learning more getting-through skills without anger gets lost in the fallout.

I see this pattern as most painful in those who are habitually withdrawn, the quiet ones. Because each time they speak out in anger it backfires, then each time they try and fail they end up withdrawing further.

Even though the rest of us have plenty of evidence that getting through to each other without anger is difficult, we may neglect the need to develop the skill because we repeatedly **underestimate the difficulty.** Then it's just too easy to retreat to the safety of blaming others: "She's got a wall up. There's no getting through to her." The opposite would be to say, "Maybe there's something I can work on... my own skill... something I don't see now."

Before I go further, I want to write about the need to learn to tell others how we feel, when we choose to. I'm very much in favor of cultivating enough skill so that we **can** tell our feelings to others so they can know us at a deeper level. But, as I've written before, I definitely believe it doesn't work for us to tell the target of our hurt and anger why we're hurt and angry (unless we want to end up ultimately isolated, "out in the cold").

Later I'll be writing about some of the reasons getting through to each other (without anger) is so difficult. But for now let's look at why the need to get through is so important that we sometimes pull out a knife (or only a needle) even when we know we'll end up with regrets.

NOT GETTING THROUGH

ANGER

From infancy, we start out being the littlest person around, so how do we cope with that? Probably at some point we have to overcome the fear that we might be **too** limited, **too** inadequate. So we spend our time trying to reassure ourselves that we're really all right. We constantly are seeking answers to our unspoken question, *"How'm I doing?"* We probably don't get direct answers, so we constantly are comparing ourselves with others.

I see most communication as testing to see if what we think and feel is accepted...even appreciated. We have such a horror of being isolated, we keep checking to be sure we aren't "out on a limb," "too far out," or maybe even "off the deep end."

We constantly seek assurance that our very real limitations aren't **too** great. We fight to get credit for what we do, and this won't happen until we can get through to others, verbally, so they **can** know us. We desperately want acceptance of our right to be the way we are, and again this rests on being able to share what we are. And we long to be respected and have impact on the world around us. We need to avoid that worst of all feelings, that we might be a nobody, and an isolated nobody at that. Unless we're able to compare notes with others, constantly, we can be completely ignored.

My summary of what we really want is this: We want others to care enough that they will make our life easier...(or at the very least, not make it harder). The word I use as a catch-all to describe what we want is **appreciation** as that encompasses the basic reasons we want so badly to get through. It's what we get from others which makes it easier to appreciate ourselves and believe we truly are all right.

Life isn't too bad if we know how to get a little appreciation, at least occasionally, and this is easiest to do if we have at least one person who consistently cares to hear us. Just being heard helps us feel appreciated, and we can believe that what we say makes some sense. Maybe what is inside us really is

NOT GETTING THROUGH

ANGER

worthy of getting out. It may even be significant, profound.

I think we all know that when we feel really listened to, we feel powerful. And it feels good to come home at night and report to a partner on the day's events and know we'll get a fair hearing. When we tell of problems, the other might respond, "Sounds like things were really tough...I don't know how you go through all that."

It helps us most if the other assumes we'll work through our own problems. When the other stays out of the way and really listens, we keep thinking of our troubles, maybe figuring out what we'll do about them tomorrow. We may ask for suggestions at some point, or maybe we won't. **But we**

ourselves take the lead in problem solving...and the other knows we'll handle our own thoughts and feelings.

The opposite occurs when couples are habitually angry. Saying, "Things were really rough at work today," would bring on a predictably heated exchange: "You told me all that yesterday. I told you to quit that job." (The meaning seems to be this: "What you have to do to be accepted by me is to do what I tell you to do.")

It's easy to see that the number one barrier to getting through is anger, in all its forms.

□

Chapter 9

*Realizing we can't completely understand...
anyone!*

Now I'm going to shift gears a little ... maybe a lot. I'm thinking of our feeling that we can't get through, and how this often leads to anger. And I'm posing a question: What if we can't **ever** really get through and really be understood? Wouldn't it follow, then, that the more we hold onto the belief that we ought to be able to get through (and be understood), the more we'd be angry?

It isn't that we would ever give up **trying** to get through. But if we're going to shake the anger habit, I think it's important to realize that we won't **ever** make it all the way to real understanding. Unless we learn to **accept** less and **expect** less getting through, we'll probably continue to form anger.

Let's look at some of the reasons we can't really get through more than occasionally. First, we'll say I want to share what's going on with me, and I talk as fast as I can. I can't possibly tell you enough for you to really understand me, as my speech is too slow and my thoughts and feelings come too fast. And you wouldn't want to hear so much anyway, as then you wouldn't be able to have space for a thought of your own.

So how do we relate? Maybe we each take two percent of what's going on with us and share. Both of us still continually have to guess about what we don't know, as it's humanly impossible to check all our guesses. And it's nearly impossible to be sure which are facts and which are guesses.

So we can **never** really know what's going on with another, for sure.

It's inevitable, when we start making better observations, that we'll be talking to ourselves and each other more accurately. We'll be learning and re-learning the need for watching every word we say. That's because it really isn't easy to say what we mean, for all kinds of reasons. Just one is that the language itself has tremendous limitations.

It's interesting that the Hopi Indians have a built-in factor which our language lacks. From what I understand, sentences containing active verbs give a cue (in the form of the verb used) to show if each statement is an eyewitness account, information gained from another, or an assumption. What fascinates me is that a people so concerned with accuracy of speech (obviously wanting to avoid misunderstandings) are called "the peaceful ones." They have one of the oldest continuous cultures in North America.

Can it be a coincidence that a people so interested in accuracy of speech have found ways to live in peace, ways that have obviously eluded the rest of us?

A primary reason we really can't get through very often comes from our being human. That guarantees that our perceptions are narrow, **much narrower** than we enjoy acknowledging. Even what we think of as within our usual range of perception actually isn't.

Consider our own noses, for example, which are always within our range of view. Yet our brain is constantly blocking them out of sight so we can focus on other things.

When I walk across the floor with a movie camera, the picture comes out jiggled. But when I walk across a room, even though my eyes are similar to a movie camera, I'm not aware of the jiggles. Why? The brain is constantly adapting, but we aren't even aware of its doing so.

Maybe you've been walking in a field in the evening and someone says, "Do you hear those frogs croaking?" When you stop and listen you're amazed that you hadn't heard the frogs earlier.

It's terribly important, when taking a wider look at anger, to realize that we can't ever really know, and understand, more than a **small portion** of what's going on at any one time.

At some level, I think we're working on our own personal system of understanding the world **all the time**. We're busy trying to integrate a lifetime's experiences with our current observations. So we're always developing our own point of view, often called a frame of reference. About all we know for sure is that no two systems of understanding can ever be alike. Our tremendous quantity of observations, thoughts, feelings and theories collected from childhood can never add up the same as another's.

Why we need to remind ourselves of this, I can only guess. Sometimes I think that in order to feel safe, we want to conclude that **most** people see things **mostly** our way. Maybe we choose to believe this in order to perceive the world as a little less scary. We desperately want to believe that if we try hard enough, we have the power to understand what's going on.

At least one thing seems clear to me: We can never be an expert on anything except our own point of view.

I wonder what you think of my version of the word "understand." We'll say I have my frame of reference over here, and there is a little niche open. You tell me something, and I say, "I understand," meaning that what you said seems to fit into the niche in my system of understanding.

But what's really happening? Maybe later you'll do something and I'll say, "That boggles my mind ... It never entered my head that you'd do something so crazy." Then I'd have to admit that I didn't "understand" at all what was happening *from your point of view.*

I think it's interesting that so many people try to avoid criticism to the extent that they try to be perfect. Yet how can one ever be perfect *except from one's own point of view* (as what makes perfection is a matter of taste).

Before I leave the point that we can't really know and understand each other, or always be aware of what we don't know, I'll give two examples.

Maybe you're familiar with the Scottish song, "Loch Lomond," in which the familiar chorus is "You'll take the high road and I'll take the low road, and I'll be in Scotland afore ye."

I've sung this song all my life and it never occurred to me to ask what it was about. Now I find the true story.

Two Scottish soldiers were taken prisoners in England, caught on the wrong side of the battle line. One was to be executed and the other sent back to Scotland.

The one to be executed was a fiddler, and he composed and sang "Loch Lomond" on the day of his execution.

All I needed to know to understand the song is that many Scotsman believe that wherever in the world they are at death, their soul goes directly to Scotland ... "You'll take the high road (by way of life) and I'll take the low road (by way of death) ... and I'll be in Scotland afore ye..."

Here is another example of my not knowing what it was that I didn't know, and in this case it caused me considerable embarrassment. I found myself on the stage of an auditorium wearing a sweatshirt and my newest Adidas, playing in a symphony orchestra with women who were wearing long evening dresses. Impossible? Ridiculous? How could I possibly have been so stupid?

I'd heard about "pops" concerts since early childhood when the term didn't mean anything. (Probably this was about the time I was singing "My country tis-a-vee.") Anyway, I went through most of my life never even wondering what a "pops" concert was.

When I started playing in a symphony orchestra (after being away from music for many years), a flyer came out before the concert suggesting that we should wear our "pops" clothing. I assumed that meant funky, just for fun, as I knew we were playing lighter-than-usual music and our formal black symphony gowns weren't needed.

Maybe you can imagine my surprise when I arrived at the auditorium to find all the women in beautiful pastel evening gowns. It wasn't until some time later that I realized "pops" referred to so-called popular music.

Can we even ask questions when we don't know what to ask? Can we ever ask **enough** questions **and absorb the answers,** even if we **do** realize what we don't know?

Repeatedly I see anger as coming from our own denial that we are too limited to know, or to be able to figure out (from our own narrow view) what ought to be. □

Chapter 10

Clinging to "what ought to be"

So how do angry people become so sure they can tell what ought to be?

When I was about four years old, I was having an argument with an older girl who told me that couples didn't have to be married to have babies. Naturally, I thought she was crazy, as that was the opposite of what I'd figured out for myself.

Of course I needed to believe I could learn how things work. Could I have just given up and believed I couldn't trust myself to figure things out? Could I have just accepted without a struggle that I truly was as inadequate as I secretly feared? What if I really was too limited to figure out what it seemed everyone else already knew?

All I could possibly do, to keep faith in myself, was to hang tighter than ever to my own view: "I'm right, you're wrong, you're crazy."

For some adults, this pattern continues even after they have enough experience to realize their limitedness. They say such things as this: "That's stupid ... there's no reason for that." Notice the meaning: "Since *I'm* unable to see any good reason for that, *there must not be one.*"

If you begin listening even more closely than usual to others' speech styles, you too will be finding, repeatedly, *that anger comes from pretending that we can see behind the scenes and know what* ought to be.

When couples come in for counseling, for example, usually they are absolute experts on what they think the partner *ought to be* doing.

There is nothing wrong with saying something *ought to be* if we also remember to say, "I think." That keeps our statement from being a flat pronouncement which reveals our ignorance (the ignorance of believing that from our own limited point of view we can know the only, the exact way something ought to be).

Just saying "I think" signals to a listener that we recognize there *may* be other explanations.

Unless we repeatedly remember to show in our speech style that we are aware of our limitations, we come through as an opinionated know-it-all. It's much better to form the habit of saying, "To me ... the way it seems to me ... from my point of view ..."

Otherwise we pronounce, "He's crazy," as if God and all the good guys of the world agree on what's what. It's so easy to say, "From where I sit, it sure looks crazy to me."

You're right if you think we might get tired of sprinkling our conversations with these phrases all the time. But if we don't use them **enough**, we won't be getting through. That's because others will be trying to get away.

We make trouble for ourselves every time we give this message: "I've been working on my own system of understanding every day of my life. And it's obvious that you other guys, you who come up with those dumb conclusions ... you don't know what you're talking about."

It's interesting to me that trying harder and harder to understand, **and believing we can**

understand, leads to anger.

A characteristic speech style of angry people is that they are often saying, *"I can't understand, I can't understand, I can't understand ... why? why? why? ... I wouldn't be so mad if I could just understand."* Their **ought to bes** aren't adding up. Yet they continue to believe that if they can collect **enough** information, they'll be able to say what they long to say, *"Now I understand ... at last it makes sense."*

To shake the anger habit, we'll not only be learning to talk to ourselves **about everything** more accurately than ever, but we'll become acutely aware of our own made-up **ought to be** pronouncements.

Review questions:

1) What question are we silently asking all the time? (page 45)

2) What do we mean when we say, "I understand?" (page 53)

3) How do we show in our speech style that we aren't an opinionated know-it-all? (page 58)

4) Why do children hang so tightly to their own narrow view? (page 57)

5) What one statement is most characteristic of angry people? (page 60)

☐

THE WORLD OF **OUGHT TO BE**

STUCK IN ANGER

POOR ME

WORLD OF **WHAT IS**

MOVING IN THE PARADE

AM I LUCKY

Chapter 11

Recovering fast from disappointments...
or the opposite

It's possible that the problem of our lives is living with the disappointment that we truly are more limited than we'd like to be. Maybe we aren't **ever** going to get all the appreciation we'd like to think we deserve. Maybe we aren't **ever** going to get through and understand others, or be understood by them as we keep expecting.

The illustration shows two basically different, and opposite, ways we habitually react to disappointment. We'll take a closer look at the anger trap in the next chapter, and you'll be learning exactly how to get out of the trap later. But this chapter is simply describing the two lifestyles.

You can see by the illustration that the trap is pictured by swirling lines, indicating plenty of energy but no forward motion. Maybe this is like a child throwing a tantrum (in a world of "poor me").

Outside the anger trap, the line constantly moves away, and stays away, from the anger trap ... "Am I lucky!" Just being in the **ought to be** (angry) world feeds the cycle of anger, whirling ever faster. The more **ought to bes**, the more anger. It becomes easy to be mad at the entire world for not being what we think it **ought to be**. (The angriest people actually have fantasies of seeing the world destroyed.)

Outside the trap we're in a position to be making the best possible observations. We continually try to see what's really going on. Since we're living in the only world we know, we try to find out how to enjoy it. In this position we keep reminding ourselves that everything depends on keeping our eyes open (our glasses clean).

Inside the trap our eyes are half closed with anger, so making clear observations is unlikely. Because we aren't able to see a full range of opportunities for ourselves, we stay stuck on the sidelines, outside the main game.

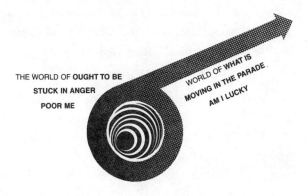

THE WORLD OF **OUGHT TO BE**
STUCK IN ANGER
POOR ME

WORLD OF **WHAT IS**
MOVING IN THE PARADE
AM I LUCKY

It's likely that we'll spend our energy pointing fingers at others who aren't doing what we think they **ought to be** doing. The parade of life seems to be passing us by, moving on and on and on. And our efforts to catch up, to get back into the parade, are futile.

Outside the trap, we keep reminding ourselves that our first job is to keep our eyes open so we can figure out how to keep on our feet. We know that only then will we be able to concentrate on our balancing skills so we can keep moving.

We can assure ourselves that it's no crime to fall down, and we don't spend time in regrets when we do. **But whenever we do fall down, our total focus is on how fast we can get up.**

Being **inside** the anger trap means that we're constantly trying to solve our problems.

But we're in a panic, trying incessantly to get the kind of changes (our **ought to bes**) we believe will make us feel better.

But what happens when we try to solve **any** problem by starting with a list of **ought to bes**? If you've studied geometry, you know you start with the **givens**. What kind of answers would you get if you started with **ought to bes**?

Failure at problem solving is guaranteed inside the anger trap (as it is based on our view of an **ought to be** world), so our painfully desired changes **aren't going to be taking place**. Yet, by the way we define our problems, we believe we won't be happy unless we get the changes. So we keep trying, but with the same methods which haven't been working (as they're still based on **ought to bes**).

Sometimes I try to describe the way I see the world **outside** the anger trap this way. Maybe it's as if we're playing in the game of life, and it is a game of cards. But when we take a good look at the cards (with our clean glasses) we notice that they are all wild cards.

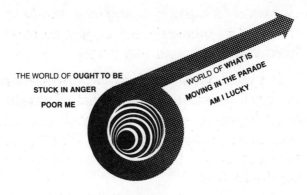

THE WORLD OF **OUGHT TO BE**
STUCK IN ANGER
POOR ME

WORLD OF **WHAT IS**
MOVING IN THE PARADE
AM I LUCKY

Each seems able to fit in anywhere and be able to move in any direction.

With human beings, since we all have minds of our own, we never can look at each other and tell, for sure, what any next move will be. So it often seems as if we're living in a crazy, wild-card world.

Just for a minute, picture all those wild-card people and notice that they insist on standing up on end most of the time. They each make keeping their balance a first priority. That's because they know that leaning over too far in any one direction might mean that they would fall and be trampled ... ending in the worst of all nightmares, out of the game.

How much energy do you suppose it would take for a wild card to stay standing up on end? Ninety-eight percent? Ninety-nine?

- What happens, in a wild-card world, if we continually call on other wild-card people for help in keeping our balance?

- What happens if we continually get mad if we can't get the help we want or expect ... or think we **ought to** get (whatever and however and by whomever we want it)?

- What happens when others aren't doing what we think they **ought to** do to help us?

- What happens every time our disappointment leads to anger? (You're right if you said, "Isolation ... out in left field again ...")

Let's look again **inside** the trap, where maybe we're saying, "I can't understand ... wouldn't **anybody** be mad when this happened?" **Just because** our view is so narrowed by our position inside the anger trap, it's easy to keep reinforcing our belief that we **ought to be** angry or hurt.

Since this leads nowhere except to more hurt, we want even more desperately to feel better. So we keep trying harder to make changes in order to solve our problems. But the "solutions" continue to be based on **ought to bes**, the ones which got us into the anger trap in the first place. At each failure we moan in real pain: "**If only** this ... **if only** that ..."

THE WORLD OF **OUGHT TO BE**
STUCK IN ANGER
POOR ME

WORLD OF **WHAT IS**
MOVING IN THE PARADE
AM I LUCKY

Because this focus keeps us from being able to see what's actually going on around us this minute (the ***what is***), we miss living. It doesn't matter which goals we achieve, sad to say. If we haven't learned how to make our ***present*** activities feel good, our "greener pastures" mindset spoils whatever we're doing.

Outside the trap, the present feels good, as our eyes are open, and we are staying on our feet so we can see in every direction. We find that keeping our balance takes very fast footwork at times, but we know that's what it takes to live in a crazy, wild-card world.

It's as if all our energy can go to staying in our own driver's seat, constantly making our own choices and correcting our course. Our job description for ourselves is narrow: keep our own balance at all times ... or we're no good for ourselves or anyone else.

But **inside** the trap, we talk about being "used," as if others are keeping us there. We "take things personally" as if the world ... and people in it ... have us in mind much of the time (rather than seeing that others are merely putting their own balance first at any given moment).

Inside the trap we keep thinking about what we think we deserve, and we look around at what others have and we truly can't understand what's going on. ("How did **they** get all that?")

We continually are saying, "I can't understand," and we keep asking "why" questions.

"**Why** does he leave me when I need him?"

"**Why** won't she listen to me (when it's obvious this is my field and she doesn't know anything about it)?

"**I can't understand why** she'd do anything so crazy ..."

As we're hurting so much from our pain, we can't accept our own (or others') limitedness. We **have** to believe things can get better. But

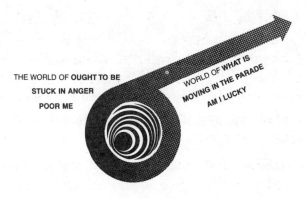

THE WORLD OF **OUGHT TO BE**
STUCK IN ANGER
POOR ME

WORLD OF **WHAT IS**
MOVING IN THE PARADE
AM I LUCKY

blaming others and denying our limitations, means that our struggle for changes (based on **ought to bes** and our denial of limitations) defeats us time and again.

The longer we stay **inside** the trap the more we feel the pain and the need to cover our pain, maybe with **dishonesty** and **exaggerations** (both to ourselves and others). Then others find they can't trust what we say, and **our struggle to get through to others, to understand and be understood, becomes even more uphill**.

Maybe we try to cover our increasing disappointment and hurt by working diligently at being a "nice guy," a do-gooder, a pleaser. Then maybe no one will suspect that we live in fear of being exposed as a "bad guy," a person who is too impossibly limited.

With this much fear, it can become a burning, constant heaviness, nearly overwhelming. If we stay in the trap long enough, we'll have an all-encompassing need for relief from pain. We'll find relief somewhere ... in spite of the long-range consequences.

This becomes a lifestyle of short cuts, zig zags and running (and all the consequences), in the hope of escaping pain, even if momentarily.

Some readers might want to argue at this point. "But wait, I'm not *always* angry. I'm not *always* in the anger trap."

But the way I see it, we don't move in and out of the anger trap because we get angry one minute and not the next. When I write about having the anger habit, I'm writing about our *tendency* to resort to anger in certain situations ... unless we've shaken the habit.

Inside the anger trap, because of our narrow vision we continue defining problems so we stay helpless:

"*If only* he'd change I'd be so happy."

"*If only* she'd come home in a better mood..."

"*If only* they'd help me more..."

"*If only* they'd appreciate what I do..."

THE WORLD OF **OUGHT TO BE**
STUCK IN ANGER
POOR ME

WORLD OF **WHAT IS**
MOVING IN THE PARADE
AM I LUCKY

Because we don't have the power to get another person to change, we stay unhappy. (Even if we tried to get the other to change by our "niceness," such attempts would meet resistance. Later I'll be writing about the way changes do come ... without either anger or "niceness.")

From our cramped view **inside** the trap, our only conclusion is that those around us just don't appreciate us **enough**. "I'll have to go it alone ... I'll never get cooperation ... no one will ever make my life easier ... poor me."

In our pain we expect rejection and we find it. We say we're afraid of making commitments as we know from experience that somehow we'll end up feeling bad, wrong, exposed as a bad guy again. Once more we'll be isolated from that wonderful closeness we fantasize about.

In this state, in our despair of **ever**

succeeding, we may have a pattern of over-reaching and falling back. Trying too hard for each impossible *"if only"* means chalking up another failure.

Outside the trap we'll be more successful in getting changes. That's because efforts are based on our most realistic look at any situation, and that includes looking closely at limitations, both ours and others'. By accepting this starting place, we are able to stay in the present. We don't need to try to escape pain by thinking up *"if onlys."*

Instead, we're in a position to be effective as we've learned to define the problems in ways which mean success (because our glasses are cleaner). And each success spills over into others.

Inside the trap *the more* we call for help and expect others (those wild cards) to come running, *the more* we're disappointed. Then we crave *even more* reassurance that we're all right (appreciated), and we hurt *even more* when we don't get it.

When others perceive us as too needy, maybe never satisfied, they may back away. We are not only triggering their *fears* of inadequacy, but their awareness of *real* inadequacy to make us happy (as that is an impossible job for someone else).

THE WORLD OF **OUGHT TO BE**
STUCK IN ANGER
POOR ME

WORLD OF **WHAT IS**
MOVING IN THE PARADE
AM I LUCKY

Something I've noticed is that when angry people become so disoriented by what other people are doing (or not doing), their anger often focuses on the need to guard material possessions ... things which are easier to manage, unlike those wild-card people. Or there may be an obsession with appearances so no one will suspect something's wrong underneath the surface.

Outside the trap maybe we'll call for help, and what do we expect? Maybe we'll get this response: "Not now, I've got to do my own thing." Sometimes we'll get help and sometimes we won't. So our comfort depends on how well we learn to live on crumbs, as that's all we'll get at times.

Inside, because we haven't learned to live on crumbs, we are in the anger trap because we truly believe we **ought to be** angry. Yet our anger itself lessens our chances to supplement the crumbs. By trying to get more of whatever it is we're trying so hard to get (by way of **ought to be** thinking), we simply increase the number of times we fail.

Outside, maybe we've come from a family tradition of belt-tightening, or whatever it takes to survive lean times with some degree of comfort. Throughout the ages people have consoled each other: "Every cloud has a silver lining ... It's darkest before the dawn."

And there's the story about the fox and the grapes, and the conclusion that since the grapes were out of reach, they probably were sour anyway.

I see it as absolutely essential, if we're to stay outside the anger trap, to learn how to handle disappointment with our limitations so we can accept the **what is**. If we can learn to focus on keeping our balance and keeping our eyes open, we'll be able to keep moving and looking for "the light at the end of the tunnel." Even seeing a pinpoint of light enables us to tip-toe ahead until we can walk more confidently. Then maybe we'll find new pathways leading off the main tunnel, pathways impossible to see in our first panic.

But when we're angry and hurting with our **if onlys**, can we relax and live on crumbs?

THE WORLD OF **OUGHT TO BE**
STUCK IN ANGER
POOR ME

WORLD OF **WHAT IS**
MOVING IN THE PARADE
AM I LUCKY

or do we become obsessed with what we don't have and what we believe we **ought** to have?

By focusing on what's missing, we're in no position to build on the **what is** in order to gain more. Yet because we **repeatedly** can't get what we think we **ought to** get, we **repeatedly** get angry and end up more isolated, with **repeatedly** less of whatever it is we think we want.

Earlier I wrote about the importance of getting through, and there is a significant difference in the way we define getting through, depending on whether we are inside the anger trap (in the **ought to be** world of "poor me") or outside in the world of **what is** and "Am I lucky!"

Outside the anger trap, because we work hard at learning how to get a fair hearing (as often as possible), we know that's **all** we can get. That's what getting through means, **by our definition.**

We stay busy comparing notes with others, and we're enjoying our getting-through skills. We're finding out we're not so unusual, so weird, or the "bad guy" of our fears. Because we can be close enough to others to successfully practice getting through, we are continually getting more and more information ... making better observations, and probably getting more appreciation. **The more comfortable we are with our balance, the more we are in a position to offer appreciation to others. We're learning to get the best out of them instead of the worst.**

Inside the anger trap, we define getting through as getting what we want, maybe convincing another to change. If I were to say, "I hurt when you do that," I'd believe I hadn't gotten through unless you stopped doing what you were doing.

If I said, "I need more appreciation," I wouldn't feel I'd gotten through unless you

THE WORLD OF **OUGHT TO BE**
STUCK IN ANGER
POOR ME

WORLD OF **WHAT IS**
MOVING IN THE PARADE
AM I LUCKY

responded by giving it (and were willing to forget keeping your own balance while trying to please me).

The problem is that with this definition of getting through (and you probably remember that not getting through can trigger anger, the knife to the heart), we have created a situation in which we're perpetuating anger.

In a wild-card world, there is little chance we'll truly get through very often in a way which fits our **ought to bes**. So we'll stay stuck with our anger, and stuck with not getting through ... which leads to more anger.

How interesting this is. If we have the anger habit, it's because we define getting through in a way which doesn't fit the **what is** (the way real people are). This guarantees that we'll rarely ever be able to get through ... in the way we expect. Then it's easier than ever to believe we **ought to be** angry.

Review questions:

1) When we're miserable and need to look away from the present by saying *"If only ...,"* how do we hurt ourselves? (page 72)

2) Give two different definitions for getting through, one we would make *inside* the anger trap and one *outside*. (page 77)

3) What are some of the age-old expressions of comfort people offer each other in times of disappointment? (page 76)

☐

THE
ANGER
TRAP

FAULTY OBSERVATIONS

FAULTY EXPECTATIONS

CATCH 22

TURN OFF POINT

HURT

ISOLATION

HELPLESSNESS

MIXED FEELINGS

ANGER

Chapter 12

Trapping ourselves with anger

In the illustration of the anger trap, you can see **FAULTY OBSERVATIONS** at the top. I believe there is one primary faulty observation which gets us into the anger trap, and it's this: "I **ought to** get more appreciation." We could express this in an endless number of ways:

> "If you cared enough for me, you **ought to** ..."

> "He **ought to** to see how much I've done for him ..."

> "She **ought to** want to make my life easier ..."

> "Because I do it this way, you **ought to** do it too ..."

"The boss **ought to** listen to me instead of those other guys..."

Whatever our choice of words, to get into the anger trap **we simply make up the belief that we're not getting enough appreciation.** (We evidently haven't been able to get through in order to get appreciation, as by our definition, that would mean being able to convince others they **ought to** give more.)

Let's look at the **what is** for a minute, the base line for any problem solving. How much appreciation are we now getting? Obviously that amount, whatever it is, is all that others are choosing to give us ... willingly.

So every time we make it up that we really **ought to be** getting more appreciation, by definition, that's a faulty observation. It doesn't jibe with the **what is**.

Once inside the trap we move easily from **FAULTY OBSERVATIONS** to **FAULTY EXPECTATIONS**, then on to **HURT**. Some people automatically move to **HURT** (maybe due to a family tradition) whenever they don't get what they expect (the appreciation they believe they **ought to be** getting).

THE ANGER TRAP

FAULTY OBSERVATIONS

FAULTY EXPECTATIONS

CATCH 22

TURN-OFF POINT

HURT

ISOLATION

HELPLESSNESS

MIXED FEELINGS

ANGER

If this has been our childhood habit, we can choose to hurt about nearly anything. It's simple. Whenever we process information to believe we **ought to be** hurt, we will hurt.

But you'll be seeing how ugly the anger trap gets as each step moves to the next, and I think you'll find the **TURN-OFF POINT** (see illustration) will look better and better.

Yes, there truly is a **TURN-OFF POINT**, and it is between **FAULTY EXPECTATIONS** and **HURT**.

Every time we don't get what we expect, we can form the habit of instantly going back and re-checking our observations: "What's wrong with my observations that I keep expecting this and getting that?"

Immediately we're back with our eyes open, outside the trap, working on our observations. We're not helpless as we're talking to ourselves as accurately as possible. We're back in the moving parade.

To stay inside the trap, we'd have to be telling ourselves something which would prolong the hurt: *"If only* she really cared *enough*, she'd be doing what I want ..."

But this is all we know for sure: She (whoever she is) *isn't* doing what we expect. So *our* problem is to keep our own balance so we can keep moving.

The only way we could stay hurt would be to believe that we *can* know what any person *ought to be* doing. We would have to pretend that we could see behind the scenes.

It takes practice, but we can learn to recognize our made-up *ought to bes*.

"She told me she'd be here, so she *ought to be* here."

"She's trying to avoid me and she *ought to* tell me the truth."

"She *ought to* call if she's going to be late."

"I deserve better treatment than this ... if she hates me she *ought to* say so."

FAULTY OBSERVATIONS

FAULTY EXPECTATIONS

CATCH 22

TURN-OFF POINT

THE ANGER TRAP

ISOLATION

HURT

MIXED FEELINGS

HELPLESSNESS

ANGER

It takes recognizing the **ought to bes** to decide whether to hold onto them (and stay hurt) or not. When we start looking back and checking our observations, we're not helpless, as we're doing **something**.

Maybe we rely on old family slogans, "Make the best of what you have," or whatever we need to tell ourselves to focus on looking ahead. We can think about what we might be able to do to make things better, as we're with the **what is**. We aren't stuck in **HURT**.

It's important to emphasize that everybody doesn't have to go immediately to **HURT** after being disappointed. We **can** learn to re-check our observations. And this **can** become just as much a habit as becoming hurt and angry.

The next step in the anger trap, after **HURT**, is **HELPLESSNESS**, and this isn't perceived helplessness, but real. That's because we realize we obviously don't have the power to get the changes we think we **ought to** get (whether in ourselves or others), or we wouldn't be in the anger trap.

But no one can stand **HELPLESSNESS** for too long, and there is one sure relief. Anyone can be angry, and it's **ANGER** which gives us temporary power. And temporary power is better than helplessness. Maybe we can force those bad guys into giving us more appreciation.

Of course the anger habit is reinforced each time we use it. The instant relief from helplessness is too great to resist. And the hope persists that we can force others to give us the appreciation we want. Or at the very least, we can punish those who won't give it.

If our eyes were wide open we could see our real problem: *There really is no way we can get appreciation, willingly given, by the use of force.*

One characteristic we find when we're habitually angry is that we believe we have to keep fighting. We continually conclude we need to fight harder: "I should have put my foot down." This is true even though such increased fighting never seems to get us what we want.

But fear of being "out in the cold," a **nobody** (and then an isolated nobody at that), is nothing as compared to the present need to relieve devastating helplessness. And the easiest way to do it is with anger.

So we continue to seek a goal (getting willingly-given appreciation) which is impossible to reach by way of anger.

Whether **ANGER** is expressed as a big blowup or only by withdrawal, the result is **MIXED FEELINGS**. No matter how justified and inevitable the anger seems, somehow we know we're losing ground.

After the **MIXED FEELINGS** phase comes the real **ISOLATION** of anger I've been writing about. If we see ourselves going around the circle of the trap, at the point of isolation, several things happen. However we're running our lives, it hurts terribly to see that our ways aren't working. We just aren't

87

getting the warm, close feelings we want so much. So we give up. We conclude, "I'd be better off alone ... at least I wouldn't keep failing and hurting so much ... anybody would quit trying after being kicked in the teeth so many times."

Even when we get a feeling that maybe we don't know what we **ought to be** doing to make things better, it's still terrifying to think of letting go of our familiar **ought to bes**. Yet our pain is so great we feel we have to give up. We're immobilized in our terror that we won't **ever** make it. The search for relief from such pain becomes all-encompassing.

Probably the most common way of finding relief is achieved by becoming numb, turning off our feelings so we won't hurt. Of course we can't feel good feelings either, but this is better than feeling the too-intense pain. We become like zombies, apathetic, afraid anything we do will turn out wrong. We're depressed, withdrawn, isolated, indecisive, scared ... and all we can do is hide.

The search for relief can lead to alcohol/drug abuse and/or suicide. But it can also lead to the kind of irrational behavior which guarantees more pain. We alternate between lashing out and withdrawing, as **neither** seems to make things better. So what does it matter which we do? Those around us

THE ANGER TRAP

FAULTY OBSERVATIONS

FAULTY EXPECTATIONS

CATCH 22

TURN-OFF POINT

HURT

ISOLATION

HELPLESSNESS

MIXED FEELINGS

ANGER

are becoming increasingly uncomfortable however, and are moving even further away.

One woman who came to me for counseling had a problem of being depressed and burying anger. She'd been repeatedly encouraged to get her anger out, and she said this: "It's better that my husband feels ten minutes of my anger every day than I be depressed."

I was appalled at the statement, and I ask you: Did the woman help herself?... or her husband?

Did the ten minutes of anger at her husband (for not doing what she thought he **ought to be** doing) make anyone feel better? (Only if you count her temporary release of tension could the answer be yes.)

But did her outburst do anything to relieve her depression ... or lessen the grip of the anger trap?

Did her husband need to know of her *ought to bes* for him? or would he be inclined to react with guilt, defensiveness, rebellion or futile attempts to please?

The biggest problem of being **ISOLATED** is that the isolation feeds our need to hang more tightly to what we know ... yet we want to give up at the same time.

Maybe the world of our *ought to bes* becomes more and more a fantasy, a desperate refuge from too much pain.

Now we're in a **CATCH 22** situation. Because we're isolated, we're in no position to get accurate information in order to be effective in problem solving. We can't combat **FAULTY OBSERVATIONS**, the kind which keep us whirling around inside the anger trap, from a position of isolation. Who will stay close to us if we will not listen?...if our *ought to bes* are so solidly fixed that we can't participate in an ordinary discussion? So how can we get information about the world around us ... how it works, the *what is?*

Review questions:

1) What is the one **FAULTY OBSERVA-TION** which gets us into the anger trap? (page 81)

2) Why is the HELPLESSNESS we feel inside the trap real? (page 85)

3) Do you believe it can ever feel good, long range, to control another with our anger?

4) Is it ever helpful to tell others our *ought to bes* for them ... even if we're operating out of our best intentions? (page 89)

☐

SECRET PASSAGE

Chapter 13

Feeling safer with ourselves... and others

When we consistently are making better observations, **we discover something we were never able to see from inside the anger trap.** And seeing this something is so crucial to getting out of the trap that I don't think we can get out and stay out until we learn about it.

Yet this section of the writing gives me trouble, as I'm so familiar with this that it's hard for me to realize how totally foreign it is for many readers.

To review just a bit, you've already seen that anger forms its own trap, as once inside, everything reinforces our staying in it. As you probably remember, I suggest taking the **TURN-OFF** *before* coming to **HURT, HELP-**

LESSNESS and **ANGER**. That means forming the habit of re-checking our **FAULTY OBSERVATIONS** *every time* we're disappointed.

And we start with the fact that even making our best observations isn't enough for us to really know what's going on (whether with ourselves or others). And being human means we're all so tremendously complicated and limited, we have to live by a mass of guesses. Yet we seem to be compelled to try to make better and better guesses, repeatedly checking them out. We desperately are trying to learn *enough* about this wild-card world that we can make *enough* sense that we can live with confidence.

You can see that what we need is a way of processing *all* information, a guideline which makes everything look different and also makes *all* of our goals reachable. ("Impossible!" you say? Read on.)

This will make more sense if you see the problem as figuring out *how* to make our glasses cleaner, learning *how* to get ourselves into a position so we *can* make the kind of observations which give us a chance of learning how to conduct ourselves better.

This rests on becoming comfortable enough

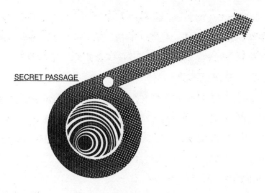

SECRET PASSAGE

with **ourselves** that we don't need to push and pull others in order to keep our balance. Then we can stay in a position from which to get accurate information. (Others sense safety from criticism and our former neediness, and they are willing to stay close by.)

What is it that fills all these requirements?

Sometimes I describe the route for getting from inside the anger trap to the outside as a secret passage. But it is only secret because so few people seem to know about it. I think it's there in plain sight for all to see ... when we are comfortable enough with ourselves that we **can** open our eyes without fear of what we'll find. Only then can we make better and better observations of **what is**, as well as learn how to get more and more appreciation ... and be able to give it.

My conclusion, after listening for thousands of hours in the counseling room, is this: Taking the secret passage rests on the awareness that all of us truly are doing the best we can, all the time, just trying to keep our own balance.

"But wait a minute," you say, "how do I **know** we're doing the best we can all the time ... just trying to keep our balance?"

I can't know for sure, so I made it up. No matter what theory I once might have had (from my own frame of reference) about another's behavior, I know it's only one of many guesses I might make. Since I no longer am pretending to know what's behind the scenes, I realize I can't know what information another is processing.... or how the other is struggling to keep balanced ... at this minute. So I choose to believe that each person is doing the best he or she can ... all the time ... in order to keep their balance.

Of course I can **try** to believe that I can see behind the scenes. But I have to concede that I only **think** I know what another ought to be doing *from my frame of reference*.

Do I hear you saying, "Now wait a minute.

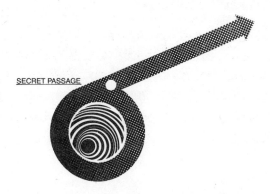

SECRET PASSAGE

Does this mean we're supposed to like everything that's happening?" Definitely not! But we **can** know that being angry doesn't help us to make things better. In fact, it makes our problem solving less effective.

Should we be willing to turn the other cheek? No, and I'm not advocating "live and let live" either. I personally am an activist and work very hard for what I believe. I'm not suggesting inaction, but I am suggesting that **acceptance** of the **what is** is the only starting place for problem solving, as it's the only **effective** position from which to make **effective** changes.

In my experience there can be no real problem solving unless this starting point is reached, an **acceptance** of the **what is**. And this point is **always outside the anger trap** (outside the world of **ought to bes**).

The best thing about choosing to believe we're all doing the best we can is that we no longer are straining so hard to understand what we can't understand. (Remember, angry people are continually saying, "I can't understand," as they can't see why their **ought to bes** aren't adding up. When we no longer are judging each other, we don't need to try to decide whether everything makes sense *from our own point of view or not.*)

Of course we'll keep trying to understand, as we seem to be made this way. But we can also be aware that we can only make it to understanding *in our own limited way* and from *our own point of view.*

Listening in the counseling room makes it easy to see that we're all doing the best we can. If I could listen long enough, I believe I'd see that each person is just trying to keep his or her balance, no matter what an onlooker might think.

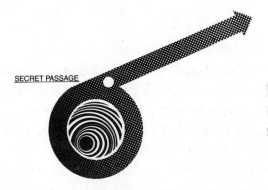
SECRET PASSAGE

My problem as a counselor is this: How do I help those who are **habitually** inside the anger trap (those with the half-closed eyes) to **ever** see out of the trap long enough to learn that we all are truly doing the best we can?

Maybe the jump out of the trap to find the **TURN-OFF POINT** rests on taking a leap of faith before we can discover the secret passage.

But how do we get to the point at which we **can** take that leap of faith so we can actually **believe** we're doing the best we can? If it were easy, I probably wouldn't be writing this book.

Maybe it would be better to ask this question: What can we tell ourselves so we function best? Does blaming and criticizing ourselves do anything except make us shrink? Or do we function better, whatever the details, when we believe we did pretty good, so we can relax and maybe do even more?

It's not easy to explain that when we stop fighting for more, things change for the better. **Then** we're in a position to rest our case and decide we're okay as we are. It's from **this** position that we can make everything better. Because we can live with crumbs occasionally, the knowledge that we're exactly like other human beings, and terribly, terribly limited, is no longer too painful to bear. We're all we've got, so where do we go with that knowledge?

Well, we can realize that we ourselves have the power to become our own judge and jury, as only we can decide what is best for us, in the long run. This comes with our daily experience in making decisions and keeping our balance. Whenever we realize that we alone can choose to see that what we're doing is all right for us ... at this minute ... it means we can take that knowledge with us whatever we do.

No matter whether it is two weeks or two years from now, we can know **in advance** that we will feel all right about whatever we're doing. **That's because we've learned how to define what we do as a success.** We simply choose to believe that we'll be doing the best we can, just trying to keep our own balance (even if our behavior sometimes seems unusual to **ourselves** as well as others).

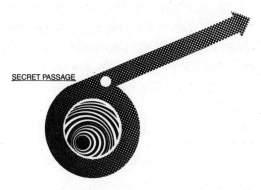

SECRET PASSAGE

Inevitably in workshops people ask me: "But wouldn't this belief just be a cop-out for doing nothing, maybe staying in bed all day?"

What an interesting question. I think you know, for yourselves, that staying in bed all day (if you're not sick) doesn't really feel good ... for long. That wouldn't be the choice of a person who is comfortable enough with him or herself to believe we're all doing the best we can ... all the time.

In fact, just the opposite is true. *If we criticize ourselves, that's when we function poorly and want to withdraw, not the opposite.*

Maybe you see that by believing we're doing the best we can, we've solved that gigantic problem: how to live gracefully with our limitations (without becoming angry and making things worse). When we choose to believe we're doing the best we can, it means we are *safe with ourselves, safe to look at ourselves, safe to enjoy living, safe to make decisions and safe to change our course when we choose.*

You'll be finding that learning how to keep ourselves *safe* is a key to all human relationships. Then others may be willing to get close... so we won't be isolated.

This doesn't mean we won't misjudge situations, and certainly fall short of what we sometimes think we *ought to be*. But then we catch ourselves. Wait, we don't know what *ought to be* (at least the final word) ... What do we really know?

If we are out of the trap, making better and better observations, we stand a chance of making pretty good guesses about what we should try next.

Even when we stay on our feet and keep our balance, of course we may go down some blind alleys. But is that still doing the best we can? Of course. Otherwise we will fault ourselves for not having the gift of foresight. Are our observations inadequate at times? Of course. Should that result in self-anger (usually called guilt)? No, and all we need do is focus on making the best of any situation. That ability keeps us going on ... and on ... and on ... still in the game.

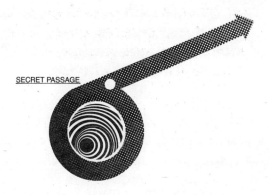

SECRET PASSAGE

This entire point, realizing that we are truly doing the best we can all the time (what I call finding the secret passage out of the anger trap) is absolutely essential to getting out. It is so crucial that I'm going to work on it some more.

When I was about ten years old, my dad disappointed me. It would seem to most people, probably, that the disappointment would have been very, very minor. And I'll later tell you what happened to cause it.

After I witnessed this thing that my dad did, I became so fouled up that I barely knew how to survive. I simply didn't know how to process the information I'd gotten. I didn't tell my mother or my brothers or sister, and I didn't talk to them about this until **over forty years later.** But in the meantime I vowed I would never let my dad see me smile and I would never look him in the eyes. This also lasted for **over forty years.**

This wasn't always easy for me, and I remember one specific time when I was in the eighth grade, wondering how I could manage when my dad had to take me to a rehearsal for a school operetta. How could I get through the evening without smiling?

I have no idea, even yet, what the neighbors thought ... or even other members of my family. Maybe it was "that bad kid," as my own perception of myself in general was that I was a pretty bad kid. (I didn't love my mother as I thought I was supposed to, just one more evidence of "badness.")

Now I'll tell you what my dad did when I was ten years old that resulted in the forty year trauma. He'd been telling everyone that he'd quit smoking, and **one time** I saw him smoking.

Of course there's tragedy here, as I certainly missed any decent relationship with my father ... and I'm sure this has affected all

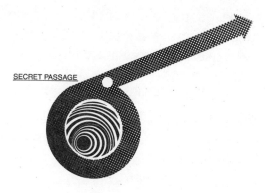

SECRET PASSAGE

my other relationships. But now I'm looking back, and I'm saying that I know now, that even with that strange behavior all those years, I was doing the best I could.

What this means is that I'm acknowledging that I don't ever really know for sure what cues I'm reacting to, internally or externally, or exactly how my mind works, or how it did when I was a child ... or will in the future. It doesn't bother me to acknowledge that I don't know, and it helps me to make some sense out of the world by concluding that all of us, no matter how strange our behavior may look to ourselves or others, are doing the best we can.

I've simply got a choice: Which belief helps me function best today? That I really was a bad little kid? or that I was doing the best I could?

I'm aware that it isn't easy for a person who

believes there's something wrong with self-acceptance to be willing to make the choice which leads to experiencing it. It's as if there is virtue in self criticism. ("I'm my own worst critic.") But self-anger fits all that has been written here about anger.

It takes a conscious effort to choose, repeatedly, to talk to ourselves in ways which make self-acceptance possible.

But are **others** doing the best they can? We start with the fact that we can't see behind the scenes and check out the facts. So which guesses help us most? Could I be convinced (could I make sense from my point of view) of the fact that **others** are doing the best they can? No, I have to make it up, just as I made it up that I myself am doing the best I can to keep my balance.

When I really began to realize that we're all doing the best we can, I could see that others were feeling safer around me. For one thing, I wasn't so obsessed with trying to understand everything, and I quit asking so many questions (changing a lifelong habit).

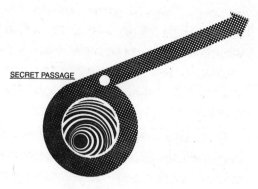

SECRET PASSAGE

People usually do feel safe with me now, and I'm able to get more and more information (and make better observations).

The world **does** seem to make more sense when I have thousands of pieces of the puzzle of life and am still getting more, than when I had only a few too-well-worn pieces.

How do I talk differently now ... both to myself and others? How do I define problems so they are more workable? How do I make sure I feel good about myself, no matter what I do?

For one thing, remembering that we're all doing the best we can all the time, means that we talk in kinder language. To me, that just means we talk more accurately.

We see another person doing something which seems strange, maybe angrily pushing people away. Instead of thinking, "How bad, how crazy that guy is," I'd think something like this: "He really must be desperate to be pushing people away like that."

From my point of view, this makes what goes on around me make **enough** sense that I can focus on what's ahead. Whatever it is that I find ahead, I know I need to look closely at it to stay in the game and keep moving.

Repeatedly there's an awareness that it's keeping my balance which takes first priority. To regain my balance, fast, I concentrate on what **I'm** going to do, **my responses** to whatever is going on. I don't need to be looking at anyone's "badness" to explain what's happening.

It feels wonderful to be completely unhooked from the endless "why" questions. Learning to say **"I think"** when I'm talking about what **ought to be** makes all the difference. I've broken the automatic mindset which leads to anger. And I've found the secret passage that keeps me out of the anger trap. □

Chapter 14

Practicing a new habit (instead of bringing anger home with the groceries)

Pat Rooney used to work out of town, coming home only for weekends, and he'd follow the same sad pattern each time. He would get angry at his family when he first arrived and the damage would last until Sunday afternoon, time to return to work. Here's what would happen.

Each Friday afternoon before he'd get on the freeway to drive home, he'd go to a specialty market to buy the choicest groceries with each family member in mind. He'd be enjoying the process fully, anticipating each enthusiastic response for his perceptive choices. The more delicious the groceries, he figured, the happier his family would be, and the more appreciation he'd get for his long week away and the four-hour drive home.

Upon arrival, each time he'd be surprised to find that there would be no brass band, no one running out to the car with open arms, and no one to squeal in admiration for his wonderful groceries.

So each Friday night he would storm into the house, seething with disappointment. He would find family members doing their own things, just as if his arrival was no major event.

Maybe his daughter would be doing homework, and maybe one boy would be on the phone and the other getting ready to go out. Maybe his wife would be doing a fast housecleaning while dinner was cooking.

Because each week Pat would withdraw in hurt, his only comments would come with sarcasm and criticism. Because he let his family know about his hurt and anger each week, they reacted by withdrawing from him and protecting themselves, or maybe fighting back.

(From Chapter Four you probably remember what happens when we tell the targets of our hurt and anger about our **ought to bes** for them.)

Pat would call out, "Isn't anybody going to help me put the groceries away?" Then he'd hear the scrambles: "... you help him" ... "no no, I've got to do this ... you help him."

Readers can guess the rest of Pat's story. The more his anger isolated him, the more he felt like an intruder, an outsider, unwanted in his own home. By the time the weekend was over, the specially chosen groceries would not only be forgotten, but they all seemed to have turned sour.

Careful readers probably recognize all the elements of the anger trap. Because Pat was inside the trap, all he could do was repeat to himself his familiar **ought to bes** which were keeping him helpless.

- They **ought to** see that I deserve appreciation for driving so far, fighting all that traffic and working every day to pay bills. They have no idea of what I go through.

- At the very least, they **ought to** appreciate my bringing the groceries enough that they'd want to help me carry them in.

- They **ought to be** grateful I come home at all.

- When I tell them what I want, they **ought to be** willing to help me get it.

- When I'm hurt, they **ought to** care enough to change what they've been doing.

- When I get mad, they **ought to** know I mean business. They can't ignore my needs week after week.

What Pat couldn't see was that he couldn't change the situation unless **he** changed what **he** was doing. They wouldn't react to him differently until he stopped hitting them with anger when they didn't do as he expected.

So the pattern kept repeating. Hadn't he told them last week how hurt he was? Wouldn't that mean they would treat him better this week? Didn't he have any impact on them? Couldn't he get them to make the changes he wanted?

No doubt you can spot some of Pat's **FAULTY OBSERVATIONS** and **FAULTY EXPECTATIONS**. From inside the trap, Pat

couldn't find the starting point for problem solving, as he couldn't accept the **what is**: "There's something wrong here ... *my anger isn't getting me what I want* ... each week things aren't better ... in fact my family really doesn't seem happy to see me ... obviously buying fancier and fancier groceries and expecting them to change isn't getting me anywhere."

Unless Pat could break his own mindset (*that his anger* **ought to be powerful enough to force the appreciation he craved**), he couldn't see that he needed to go back and re-check his observations. He couldn't see how he was hurting himself by continuing to believe that his family **ought to** respond to his anger by doing what he wanted. *It seemed so obvious that it was their fault that he was angry.*

It is easy to see that his anger was creating resistance, as no one wants to be controlled by another's hurt and anger. We're made so strangely that we think it's important that we make our own decisions about what we do.

Each week, inside the trap, Pat would go **automatically** and **instantaneously** to **HURT**, and Pat says this meant feeling suddenly as if "all systems were shut down." His hurt would be **so overwhelming** that it was as if everything stopped. All he'd know is that he was suddenly on the sidelines, out of the action. It was as if he never had a choice. The hurt just took over.

Then he would feel **HELPLESS**. "What else can I do? Won't they **ever** let me get through to them? Won't they **ever** consider my needs? Won't I **ever** get what I want, a warm, happy family?"

Because he couldn't tolerate such blinding helplessness, he relied on his old standby, **ANGER**, to gain the power to get through (the knife to the heart): "I'll show you ... you'd better not ignore me ... you'd better decide to do what I want next time."

In this mood, even though he knew his sarcasm would backfire, he felt compelled to let his family know of his discomfort. That seemed better than doing **nothing**, just being alone with his hurt ... hurt ... hurt.

But after each episode of hurt and anger, **MIXED FEELINGS** would follow: "I can't

make any impression on them ... I know my anger doesn't help, but they deserve it. I won't bring home any more groceries ... I'll have to look elsewhere to find a loving family."

ISOLATION was inevitable when the pain of repeated failures became overwhelming. The **CATCH 22** was that **ISOLATION** kept Pat from being able to make accurate observations of what was really going on. He knew he was triggering the **opposite** of what he wanted, but when he continued to believe he **ought to be** hurt and angry, he knew no other way to get relief except to tell his feelings to his family.

But nothing was working. The more Pat hurt and withdrew, the more he was blinded by his **ought to bes**. Stuck only with his own point of view, there was no possible way of reaching any conclusion except that his family was to blame for his problems.

Couldn't they see that they **ought to** give him more appreciation?

It took only that one **FAULTY OBSERVA-TION**, that one single *ought to be,* to guarantee that he would keep whirling around inside the anger trap.

How did Pat shake the anger habit? Did he ever learn to get appreciation for himself? and appreciation for bringing home the groceries? Did he ever figure out how to get through to his family ... at least part of the time?

Let's look behind the scenes. For Pat's transition it helped to remember that because we're all doing the best we can, we don't deserve anger. This was hard for Pat, as he was such a compulsive pleaser himself that he **expected** (falsely) that his family ought to be doing their best **to please him**.

Finally he could see that we're all doing the best we can *from our own point of view*, just trying to keep our own balance.

Taking a new look at his situation, he could see that it was unlikely his family deliberately was setting out to hurt him. In his own anger, because he often thought of getting revenge, he attributed similar thoughts to his family.

116

No, it wasn't easy for Pat to shake the anger habit. Yes, he has effectively cut the downtime of his anger.

He had to get comfortable enough **with himself** that he could make better and better observations. And what made this possible? **Reminding himself, again and again**, that all of us are doing the best we can, all the time, as that meant that he could calm down and face his **ought to bes**. He could relax enough to ask himself some different questions.

- Does it help to keep telling myself how justified my anger is?

- Has getting angry at my family **ever** gotten me what I want, more closeness?

- Are they more, or less, likely to cooperate with me after I get sullen and angry?

- How can I keep from feeling isolated so much of the time?

When Pat could break his old mindset which had been bringing him instantaneous hurt, he realized that his family members may have wanted appreciation each week *from him.* He knew he'd been buying the groceries in order to get their appreciation (as he was such a pleaser), but it didn't occur to him that *they* might also be wanting *his* appreciation.

So now he could think this way:

- What would happen, each time I arrive home, if I were to approach each person and show interest in what each one was doing ... and what they were interested in *at that minute*?

- What would happen if I were to remember that listening is an effective way of showing appreciation to another?

- How would each family member treat me if I weren't mad every time I arrive?

Sometimes, to break a mindset which leads to automatic hurt, it helps to make up guesses about what's going on. That helps us break our unflattering assumptions made from inside the anger trap.

Here are some of Pat's guesses about what might have been happening with his family.

Maybe when he arrived, each person was engaged in doing something which they thought would make the weekend better. Maybe his wife wanted the house tidy so the family could enjoy the homecoming dinner. Maybe the daughter wanted her homework out of the way in order to spend more time with her dad. Maybe the boys were taking care of their own things so he wouldn't be embroiled in their wants and needs.

That's just one guess to oppose the notion that they were deliberately hurting him. (After all, if they **really** cared, wouldn't they be running out to the car each week with outstretched arms?)

But here's another made-up theory. Maybe each family member wanted him to catch **them** in the act of whatever **they** were doing, whatever was important **to them.** (This couldn't happen if they were expected to run out to the driveway at exactly the right moment.)

What is interesting to me is that I learned, from my own experience, that this second theory had merit. And I'll tell you something important I re-learned from Pat's story, something tremendously helpful for those who are learning to shake the anger habit.

Once when Pat was to arrive at my husband's and my home to pick up his teenage daughter (after one of his four-hour drives), his daughter and I were doing some work and we had a mass of papers spread out in every possible direction.

We were very much looking forward to Pat's arrival, and I fully expected him to be happy to find that his daughter and I were so engrossed in a project we found so interesting. I certainly wasn't thinking about his experience bringing home the groceries, although he had been telling about it in seminars. So I was dumbfounded to see what happened at our home.

Neither his daughter nor I had stood up for a bear hug when he had entered, as we had just a little more work to finish so we'd all have dinner. I worked for another few minutes and walked into the living room.

To my great surprise I saw Pat sitting on the divan reading a newspaper. What had happened was that he had been so

disappointed at the reception we had given him that he had experienced, again, that terrible hurt, the kind that meant "all systems were shut down." His old habit of fearing rejection, and **believing he'd found it**, meant he had withdrawn to lick his wounds, isolating himself.

Fortunately the downtime of his anger didn't last long.

Working from my own frame of reference (the only one I have!), because I'd been so sure Pat would be pleased instead of unhappy, one thing became very clear to me. **From my own experience**, since I knew that his daughter and I had been delighted to see him, it was obvious that **only** Pat's misinterpretation of the **what is** had thrown him into his old instantaneous hurt, anger and withdrawal.

Looking back later over this situation, it's sad to think of all of Pat's anger, over all those weekends bringing home the groceries ... all due to his misinterpretations. He stayed trapped in hurt and anger because he believed he had evidence that his family didn't appreciate him **enough** (by his definition of **enough**).

All he did to change the pattern was to realize that it didn't mean his family was rejecting him because they wouldn't be controlled by his anger. It didn't mean they were against him because they didn't do as he expected. It didn't mean they deserved his anger and attempts at revenge because they were scrambling to keep their own balance in the face of his sarcasm.

It took Pat's being outside of the anger trap to be able to see that he alone had to change his mindset, and that ended his isolation. □

Chapter 15

Overcoming fear of exposure as a "bad guy"

Sometimes I think the driving force behind most of us is our fear of being exposed as a "bad guy." For some of us, maybe this means we feel ninety-nine percent "bad" ... protected only by a very thin layer of "good."

So it takes just one criticism (or frown of even imagined disapproval) to crack that thin layer and plunge us down to zero: "I'm a rat ... I've made her unhappy again ... I'd better give up ... no matter how hard I try I'll never make it."

Because most of us feel different degrees of imaginary badness inside us at different times, getting angry is one way the percentage goes up. It seems to be just one more evidence of "badness," one more reason to hurt.

Maybe you remember that on the diagram of the anger trap the **TURN-OFF POINT** is between **FAULTY EXPECTATIONS** and **HURT**. And those who *habitually* feel hurt whenever disappointed, go deeper into the trap. And those who go back, instead, to check their **FAULTY OBSERVATIONS,** they're the ones who get out of the trap.

It's easy to see, with Pat and the groceries, that it was his too-thin imaginary protection for that imaginary bad guy inside him which habitually caused his downfall. His *tendency* to believe he *ought to* hurt, came from the childhood way he'd learned to process information. And his constant hurts, his fears of *too much* "badness," often overwhelmed him.

A common method (which doesn't work) to try to calm our imaginary bad guy fears is to be a "nice guy." To avoid criticism, we think we can smile enough so that others will believe all is well. Maybe they won't notice that sometimes we feel hollow inside, or maybe full of some kind of poison. Evidently we're just not "good" enough to get the appreciation we see others getting.

In this state we'll do practically *anything* to get one stroke of appreciation to bolster that thin layer of protection. Those who "can't say no" are in this category, constantly choosing to hurt themselves while they chase after some imagined, but desperately needed stroke.

An example would be being so nice that against our wishes we'd talk to a person making a sales pitch on the telephone. We'd be totally unable to simply hang up after saying, "I really don't want to talk now."

Another example of too much "niceness" (coming from the fear that someone somewhere **might** have a bad thought about us) comes when the phone rings. Maybe we answer it and someone says, "I've been trying to get you all day."

Instead of being quiet and waiting to see what was so urgent, the "nice guy" goes into great detail to explain all the **good** reasons he or she was unable to answer the phone. "I had to go to the bank ... then take the cat to the vet ... and the vet had an emergency..." This becomes a lifestyle marked by habitual defense of our "niceness," as if we're continually saying different versions of this: "I don't want you to think that I'm bad because I couldn't read your mind and know you'd be trying to call me."

An interesting thing about "nice guys" is that they are especially afraid of **others'**

anger, as it might trigger their own which they are so desperately trying to keep hidden.

Here's an example of "niceness" being carried to a point of real danger. A friend had such an unpleasant experience while driving that she briefly considered staying home forever after. She'd been especially tired one night and missed seeing a stop sign. Fortunately her error had caused no trouble at all, not even a near accident.

But another driver had seen what she'd done and became enraged. He began to yell at her and follow her home. At each turn, as they got further and further away from town, the more uncomfortable she became.

In her disorientation she stopped and went back to talk to the other driver who had stopped his car when she did. (Naturally she assumed her "niceness" and logic would carry the day.)

But the conversation wasn't very pleasant. And, except for her feeling that maybe she'd never leave the safety of her home again, no tragedy occurred.

But why did she risk such danger to herself by getting out of the car to talk to a hostile stranger?

She says she felt the need to get him to acknowledge that what she'd done really hadn't been **too** bad.

One of the problems, if we think we have to be "nice" all the time, is that we can't be honest because we're too afraid of inflicting real or even imaginary hurts on others. Usually we justify our distortions by saying that we don't want to hurt anybody. And this may be true, but let's look closely.

A young man phoned me to ask if I'd seen his girlfriend who works out of town. He said he'd been afraid to leave the house as he was expecting her to call saying she was coming over. So he'd stuck by the phone all day, even though all day he'd been wanting to go and work out at the gym.

I told him that I was pretty sure his girlfriend planned to be out of the area for some time.

Knowing her, it appeared to me that she hadn't been able to tell her friend the truth. It was a good guess that she was too afraid of the pain **she'd** feel (even if only briefly) at *seeing* his hurt if she'd told him she'd be gone for awhile.

Was she really afraid of hurting **him** (as she probably told herself)? Or was it her own fear of *seeing* his hurt (which could have triggered her own "bad guy" feelings)? ... and this fear of her own "bad guy" was so great she was willing to risk hurting him **much more** (but only while he was safely out of her sight)?

What is sad is that whatever our motives, all the getting-through efforts of **habitually** being a "nice guy" or a pleaser, may mean that we are **habitually** dishonest. For our listeners the details don't quite fit, and this is discomforting to them sooner or later ... no matter how clever we think we are.

The more we try to "protect" another from the truth, the more discomfort for them.

The more we fear another's anger, and don't quite tell the truth, the less chance we have of getting through.

It's possible that we may be unaware that what we say may contribute to another's discomfort or scrambles to protect the internal "bad guy." Or, we may fear the opposite and exaggerate our power to hurt others. We may feel as if we have some kind of a "monster" in our guts that must stay hidden, that "badness" which can inflict pain. Some people talk as if they have a fatal flaw or a missing piece, but it all adds to that "something's wrong ... I must be bad" feeling.

Probably we all have different ways of dealing with such "something's wrong" fears, and in my own case, what I'll recount here is probably no more ridiculous than what other little kids are doing ... right now.

In a family of six people, it seemed to me that three of my family members were good and two of them were bad. (This was clear, as in my black and white thinking, I could easily see that one brother was a saint and the other a sinner.)

But where did I fit into the family? Terror struck my heart.

Of course there's no rule, made on high or otherwise, that a family must be evenly divided between good and bad. But **if** this were true that there **ought to be** three good and three bad, that would mean **I was bad**. So I lived in tremendous fear.

Each time we were at the dinner table I did something which made it possible to ease my terror ... slightly. Whichever way my father and the sinner had their plates arranged (the fried potatoes here, the hamburger patty there with string beans in between), I felt I had to make **certain** that the arrangement of food on my plate **didn't even look like theirs**.

As I'm writing all these years later, one thing which strikes me as sad is that I don't think it even occurred to me to look to see how the three "good guys" had arranged their plates.

Long after I was married, and my husband and I were raising our two children, it was easy for me to be controlled by my husband's criticism: **"You're not the way a good wife ought to be."**

Since I would take each criticism as a sign I should go back to zero (where I **really** belonged), it was some time before I realized that I usually ended up somewhere in the middle, maybe fifty-fifty. So I asked myself: Why shouldn't I just go to the middle in the first place and cut out all that downtime?

I finally made it, not only to the middle, but to the top. *I no longer ever feel guilty, defensive or bad.*

How did the transition come?

It's impossible to know for sure, but I do know that I used to feel as if I were blindly traveling in a fog and couldn't put my hand on the switches which would make things better. Now I feel I can find the switches, and yes, things are wonderfully better.

But it's humbling to admit that I had to go back to school, get a Masters Degree and a state license so I could listen to clients, all in order to learn how to be a good marriage partner.

Because I know how tremendously difficult this is ... and how rewarding, I have great compassion for those who haven't been able to make their marriages work. As you can guess, I feel a real desire to share what I've learned.

Mostly, I know that we all desperately want to be *safe, safe* from criticism, *safe* from the fear that our cover of "good" might fail us. That's why we want appreciation so badly, the reassurance from others, preferably, that whatever package we come in, it's **all** acceptable. And we want such appreciation **especially** when we fear that maybe we've been **too** stupid.

Because we know we want this acceptance so much for ourselves, we realize we have to learn to give such acceptance to others. But how do we get into a position so we can be accepting? How do we get comfortable enough with ourselves that we can get ... and give ... appreciation?

How do we learn to run our lives so others can see we are safe enough that they **can** come close? How do we conduct ourselves so we **can** get information and make accurate enough observations? How do we make sure we **can** avoid the pitfalls of the anger trap?

One thing I learned was that I myself could decide whether I was safe with myself or not, whether I was all right through and through or full of poison. Before that, it had seemed that I either felt good about myself or I didn't. I just didn't realize I had a choice.

Late one night I was sitting on the edge of the bed, wishing I'd accomplished more during the day. This thought came over me: What if most people feel the way I do? What if most of us always want to be more, do more? What if we're mostly alike, in that we live our lives being limited and raging against our limits?

How ridiculous that seemed. I decided that I'd just be content with what I've got and stop pushing myself to do or be more.

I knew I could continue to try harder any time I wanted to, as I'd always have that choice. Or I could merely turn around and decide I'm all right exactly the way I am. *Because* I quit pushing myself, it became easier and easier to see that I really was making it ... already. If I'm the only me I've got, why not pronounce it all right and enjoy it?

Of course this doesn't mean that I don't have my eyes and ears open ... ready for whatever comes. But I simply walked out from under *ever* feeling guilty again. I no longer am the little kid believing that if I'll just try hard enough (at rearranging my plate?) I'll pass as all right.

The way I see it, it is likely that the only way any of us get into trouble is that we try **so hard** to make it (by whatever definition we use), that we get discouraged and give up.

It's too painful to believe we'll keep trying and failing, so we stop trying. Maybe we'll adopt an I-don't-care attitude and resort to vandalism or violence. (I hope you notice that it's the way we're defining our problems which keeps us helpless: "Because I can't make it the way I think I *ought to be* able to do, I'll stay hurt and be angry.")

The best result from my learning to be an accepting person came after I realized I was reacting differently to anger *directed at me.* If my anger habit is my own thing (the result of my own **ought to bes**), that's true for others too. No longer do I have to live in fear of anyone else's criticism of me. It makes all the difference to know that each criticism simply means that I'm *hearing another's* **ought to bes** *for me.*

I don't have to worry at all. So he (or she) sees things differently from me? What else could I expect? If I've been making good observations, isn't it clear that we'll all differ in our **ought to bes** for each other? Shall I get excited because that's the way the world is made?

Could any other person possibly know the kinds of decisions I'm working on? and how I need to use my time and energy in order to keep on my feet?

Of course not. This means that I can go anywhere with confidence as I don't **ever** expect myself to be any more than I am. That's enough. I pronounce it so. Crazy as that may sound to you, it means that I can go ahead without fear (fear of **anyone's** anger) as I'll take my balancing skills with me.

When I think of how complicated I myself am, and that everybody else probably is as complicated, I'm amazed ... and grateful ... that we relate as smoothly as we do.

The most wonderful bonus for not feeling guilty or defensive is that the "bad guy"

doesn't live here any more. So I'm **comfortable enough with myself** that others can get through to me. I'm no longer afraid of what I'll hear (as I was much of my life) or that someone will step on a sore toe.

Those talking to me can feel powerful and know they have impact, as I *want* to listen. I know my own safety lies, in part, on my ability to get information and find out how the world really works ... from different points of view.

Years ago I remember thinking that there had to be something wrong with me because life was so difficult. Now in the same world, when my first job description is simply keeping my own balance, **everything is different.**

Am I selfish? Not at all, as it's from this position that I'm most able to be cooperative, warm, sensitive and accepting.

No matter how I look at all this, it appears that tending to our own balance is the greatest favor we do for ourselves and others. Then we don't need to get mad because **others** aren't making our lives easier, propping us up or helping us avoid "bad guy" feelings.

We don't need to get mad because we're in a wild-card world... and it's impossible to stack a deck of wild cards, much less keep them stacked.

Instead, because we're keeping our balance, *we're in a position to be getting the best out of others*. They feel safe and comfortable with us because we aren't pushing and pulling them to go our way because we think that will make us feel better. *We can truly respect their need to concentrate on keeping their own balance.*

I learned something suprising from the woman who first suggested that I write about the way I handled anger. She'd been telling me that's what it was which made my counseling different. She'd been especially impressed because she was one of those who talked about having a "monster" inside her, the imaginary badness she'd had all her life.

Both of us were amazed that when she got her anger down (after three counseling sessions) that her *imaginary monster disappeared.* (That was three years ago, and she tells me the monster never returned.)

How can we make sense of this? Fortunately I don't need to understand what I can't understand. It's enough for me to know that the kind of information about anger in this book can have an exciting part in banishing monsters. And this applies to all kinds of imaginary fears of badness, the "something's wrong" feelings that keep so many of us defensive and afraid to live.

I'm willing to celebrate.   □

Chapter 16

Building closer relationships

In this final chapter, I'll report what happens in the counseling room as a means of showing how two people can learn to build warmth and closeness.

But two disclaimers first.

This isn't to suggest that you will need counseling in order to use the information here. But it's just easier for me to write about what I see every day, and then you'll decide where to go from here.

The second disclaimer is to combat the myth that it takes two people to work on a relationship. That myth makes so much sense it's no wonder so many people believe it. But I know from my work here that I get tremendous reports from **one** person who has made changes for him or herself. Then a partner who has never entered the counseling room becomes (magically?) completely different (or so it seems).

No doubt you know that changes come when we change our part so others have something different to respond to. We may be easily getting the same changes we fought for so futilely. The old patterns can't exist if even **one** person is different. (And at first this difference **only** need be in our heads, as just thinking differently is the first step.)

I'll be writing about our need to find a sanctuary, an accepting place in which we can feel safe, safe enough that fears of bad guys can be forgotten.

This means I'm back to discussing how to get through without anger (as often as possible), and I'm feeling my own limitedness just now. Every day I'm so deeply involved in helping people learn to get through (whenever possible), that writing seems so inadequate. That's because I know that getting anger down is just the **beginning** of learning to get through ... and all the practice (while wearing our clean glasses) is ahead.

I'll have to be content now with just making some generalizations and exaggerations about the way a couple learns to get through to each other. In Supplement #2 you'll find some additional suggestions for getting through, and in Supplement #3 you'll see an account of the way a relationship goes downhill and back up again.

When a couple calls in for counseling, I agree to see each person separately at first. These are two-hour sessions and I may do nothing but listen for the first hour and a half. Initially I'll say as little as possible, maybe something like this: "Just tell me what you want me to know." Because I keep my head down in my notebook I don't give any feedback if at all possible.

Usually each person comes in for two such appointments before the couple is ready for a joint session.

This is what I'll probably hear.

- Both believe they know what the other **ought to be** doing.

- Both are defining their problems so they stay helpless (... believing the other **ought to** change).

- Both live in fear of the other's anger (disapproval, withdrawal, rejection) so both are defensive most of the time.

- Both are in no position to see the partner at his or her best.

- Both try desperately to understand their problems (which to them means deciding where to place blame).

- Both feel they are "walking on eggs" when the partner is around.

- Both are in a weak position to be learning about becoming accepting: "I've got to accept *that?*"

- Both believe, at a deep level, they've tried everything.

- Both are mad that they can't get help from the other. (But when both are hanging onto the edge of a cliff by their fingernails, does it help to be mad at the other for not lending a hand?)

In spite of all the two people have in common, there is one major difference: **one is dominating and the other is withdrawing.** They may switch positions part of the time, but they stay in a one-up/one-down pattern. What they have in common is their inability to relate to equals.

Just to keep the language simple, we'll assume the dominant one is a wife, and the withdrawing one is a husband (and remember I'm exaggerating).

Because the wife is trying so hard to feel good about herself (to keep her imaginary bad guy out of sight), she may have a tendency to exaggerate her belief that she is actually one-up, at least better than her partner.

After all, she's calling the shots, isn't she? She's doing practically everything (with no help from the other, as she sees it). The more problems, the harder she works. She keeps attempting to please her partner (probably the way her mother did). She's overly helpful without realizing it's a constant put-down to the other: "I'm strong and you're weak."

She'll do nearly anything to avoid her husband's anger, as the cover for her imaginary bad guy is too thin to withstand the faintest criticism. That's because she's trying **so hard** to get acceptance and appreciation.

Not getting what she expects, she stays hurt, helpless and angry. ("**Anybody** else would appreciate me ... what's the matter with this villain? ... always somewhere else when I need help.")

She may keep herself numb in order to

avoid her pain, so she becomes more and more insensitive to her surroundings. She's probably unaware how she's stepping on toes.

She truly doesn't know how to get cooperation from her partner. And she can't understand why she's so often isolated and left to feel that she alone is holding up the world. And she not only isn't getting credit for it, but she's receiving kicks instead.

Let's look at the husband, who probably learned from his father to fear a woman's disapproval. He too may be a pleaser, or one who has given up pleasing and has become a spoiler. But he still desperately wants acceptance and appreciation.

The more his partner plays one-up, the more he feels one-down ... small, overwhelmed with "badness." He even more desperately tries to please a strong woman as he continues to believe that he *ought to be* able to please her *enough* so she will make him happy.

But since he's relied so much on a strong woman (all his life), he's probably failed to develop a variety of skills for himself. So he automatically avoids situations which expose fears of possible failure (fears of failing at pleasing ... which he probably doesn't realize is an impossible job).

He may become nearly unable to make decisions, so strong is his fear of risking the other's disapproval (the one he believes he's totally dependent upon).

Usually he just goes along with his wife, but when he knuckles under too much, he hates himself. So nowhere does he feel really safe from his "bad guy" feelings (either going along with her or standing up for himself). He concludes that his only safety is doing nothing. But he also gets criticized for that.

He hurts so much he's nearly insatiable for reassurance from the other that he's all right. Particularly after an angry outburst, he's terrified that he will be unaccepted ... out in the cold ... isolated. He often wants to make love after an angry tirade in order to get reassurance, but his wife is too upset to cooperate. She's in a state of shock from what she's just heard, the kind of poison that he's living with (probably coming from his belief that she's the chief villain in his life).

So what can I do after listening? Because I hear so many hundreds of people, with only the details different, in the individual counseling sessions it's easy to tell each person what's probably going on with a partner. (The person who has just left the counseling room may have been in the opposite position.)

As you can guess, I'm trying to combat the fact that angry people become tightly locked in the anger trap, a prisoner of their own **ought to bes**. At worst, the two people seem to be in different worlds, as anger is keeping each one from being able to listen deeply to the other.

All I do at first is talk as accurately as possible to each person about what I see. In a relaxed setting, both can see that they are barely keeping their balance because of fear of the other's anger.

I help them get more of a sense of their own and their partner's limitedness, maybe suggesting different interpretations of what they see. It's no surprise that nearly all behavior may look crazy to an angry partner (**especially** if he or she is in desperate need of blaming the other to divert attention from themselves).

At some point they can see that their ways of defining problems and finding "solutions" are leading nowhere. Because they truly have tried everything they know, they are at a dead-end. They see nothing ahead except helplessness and anger.

When they realize they have nothing to lose by choosing to believe that we're all doing the best we can, they can see this leads to hope ... a very welcome change.

Eventually they begin to see how they themselves can be triggering the reactions they are getting. In order to see this, it helps to be believing they are doing the best they can. They **really** aren't stupid because they don't know any more than they know.

For the woman I often recommend reading "The Wendy Dilemma" by Dan Kiley. (Sometimes of course the Wendys are males.) Reading at least the first part of the book helps increase awareness of dominating and feeling overly-responsible for others' thoughts, feelings and actions.

I'm busy helping the woman become more aware of her own feelings so she can talk to her-self and her partner more accurately. I'm trying to help her break the habit of talking about problems in terms of what other people **ought to be** doing.

For the husband, my listening to him at a deep level helps him realize that he's doing the best he can. He's learning that it's the way he's been defining problems which has been keeping him helpless. When he unloads his guilt (over failing to achieve his made-up **ought to bes**), he begins to function better.

It's my job to prepare each for the joint session by helping them learn more about how to talk so the other won't pull away. Ultimately they have to be able to find **comfort** from each other when they are comparing notes on **their own struggles** (in a wild-card world). It's been only the inability to find comfort in their attempts to get through which has been the problem (by my definition).

They tried to get through to each other but simply didn't know how ... then their anger made things worse. Probably there were times when one would want to talk and the other wouldn't (or couldn't). This would be dangerous, as you remember that not getting through can lead to anger. Particularly if one person is numb, and the other is trying to get through and can't make it, there's the potential for violence.

Maybe you've noticed that such fights may end up over car keys, as one or the other tries to escape. Usually it's the one prone to violence, who fears his or her own anger, who knows it's necessary to get away. But the other objects.

When two people are willing to come in for counseling, I assume their goal is to feel good about **themselves** when they're together. They know they want closeness, but they're aware they don't know how to get it.

(At least this is a notch ahead of believing the all-American myth that it's just a matter of looking harder to find the **right** partner.)

It's interesting that the purpose of the joint session is **only** for the two people to learn to hear each other (and respond to show real hearing, especially of feelings) and be able to talk so the other will listen. That's all. But that's enough.

When the strain of not being able to get through is behind them, **everything is different**. There's no immediate need for problem solving about specific issues. Rather, it's more and more apparent that it's been **only** the inability to get through (without resorting to anger) which has been making all other problems seem worse.

Part of the learning is getting a deep sense that each of us is working on our own struggles **full time**. We don't need to know each other's feelings or understand each other. **But we do need to know that for each of us, our feelings matter more than anything.** Feeling good about ourselves and keeping our balance is a necessity if we are to relate from a position of equality (or at least narrow the up/down gap).

We find we hurt ourselves when we push others to do what we want them to. And we find that for all of us, we either make our own decisions or we risk feeling like a nobody, a non-person, a zombie.

And of course it's impossible in the real world for any two people to grow at the same rate, or always in the same direction (no matter what a partner's expectations).

Yet we all seem to want the same thing, acceptance by others of our right to be struggling, *exactly* where we are at this very minute ... and that may mean being flat on our face in the mud.

So how do we learn to relate as equals ... especially after lifetime habits of feeling one-up or one-down? How can we feel good about a partner... and ourselves?

At the end of the first individual session with each partner, I give out the material found in Supplement #3, and I also do a relaxation exercise to help integrate the feedback I've given. (It's been a shorter and more personalized version of the kind of information you're finding here.) Maybe after the second session I'll give out a copy of "The Anger Puzzle." (That's Pat's and my earlier book, and from now on I'll probably give out this one.)

In the joint session I'll ask the husband to make a short statement to his wife about something he feels strongly about. It's my job to help the husband talk so his wife doesn't want to escape (mentally if not physically).

I help the husband learn to say how he's feeling without offending her: "I get so scared

you won't hear me that I'm afraid to talk."
(Earlier he might have said, "You never listen
to me ... you're bad, bad, bad..." and
wondered why the other feared being around
him, even when he wasn't, at the moment,
planning to say anything mean.)

While the wife is listening to her husband's
statement, it's her job to keep feeling good
about herself. On a scale of one to ten, that
means she's staying at a ten. Whenever she
loses her ten, we stop everything until she
regains it.

The wife's part, every time her husband
tells about his feelings, is to respond to show
she's really heard him: "Sounds like you're
terrified," (or she uses whatever word
summarizes the feelings). At each of her
responses, if her tone and body language
show genuine hearing, the husband feels
relief. (Usually I have to help her with this.)

But because she's showing real hearing, her
husband is no longer in a panic, futilely trying
to get through to her. He's able, instead, to dig
down into himself and tell her how he really
feels. Because he's no longer hitting her over
the head with every word, she's willing to
listen.

What's interesting is that if I can help his
wife stay at a ten long enough, the husband

will work all the way through his feelings from A to Z. It's **his** feelings he's talking about, and he's lived with them before, and he'll be continuing to live with them. ***But it gets easier just because he's been heard.***

The only way the wife could mess up his working all the way through his feelings would be to believe she's responsible. If she is defensive and believes **she** could change **herself** in order to make everything better **for him**, that would hurt them both. He too might buy into the assumption that it's her fault he feels the way he does.

As you can guess, later in the joint session the wife gets her turn to get a deep hearing from her husband.

Although no problems are being solved, each person feels better ... just because of the hearing and knowing he or she **can** talk in ways that get through ... at least sometimes.

This may not seem earth-shattering as you read it, but it is. Learning how to get anger down in advance (in the individual sessions) is what makes the joint session go so smoothly.

Maybe the couple will want a second joint session or maybe I won't hear from them until six months later, calling in for a check-up.

What makes the difference (and I see black and white changes between the first and third sessions) is that the two people have **experienced for themselves** that it's getting through that matters. They can *feel* that it's only listening that shows respect for the whole person, the whole package. It's **only** the listening which shows real caring for the struggling human being. (They may unwittingly have been delivering to each other this insult: "I like you **only** when you're a need-filler for me.")

Each person still has their own problems and feelings. But when they can share them with a person who cares about their struggle, life isn't too bad.

No longer is there focus on the need to get what they **think** they want. They can see that it was fighting for more which guaranteed disappointment (as the partner was constantly living in a climate of lack of acceptance). Yet when they quit pushing, everything became different.

It's exciting to see two people decide to become accepting of each other (and the **what is** world).

It's wonderful to know that we really don't have to go around scaring each other with our anger after all.

That alone is enough to motivate us to change our mindset so it's possible to shake the anger habit ... in our own time and in our own way.

Since any finish line would be only in our imagination, why not **enjoy the process** of shaking the habit? Let's begin celebrating **today.** ☐

Supplement #1

Some questions asked at seminars and workshops:

Q: Wouldn't you be mad if someone cut in front of you on the freeway and nearly caused an accident?

A: No, because I don't have the anger habit. In fact, when I'm in a crisis, my head is never clearer. I need all the wits I've got and I don't want them distorted with anger. (What helped me most to break the habit was remembering that I couldn't be angry unless I was telling myself things which weren't true, lies, **ought to bes.** Every time I'd get angry I'd remember this faster ... until eventually the downtime of my anger was practically nothing.)

Q: Don't you believe that anger is a good motivator to get us going to do something we wouldn't do otherwise?

A: Maybe so, but I think we'd probably be doing the wrong things, things that would hurt us in the long run. No matter how pure our motives, I think if we analyze a situation and act out of anger, we'd be triggering polarization and resistance instead of cooperation.

Q: Can't all this be taught in schools?

A: I can't see why not, and the sooner the better.

Q: Wouldn't it be dull to be without anger?

A: I think it's the opposite. It's as if all doors are open wider ... and just living every day is more and more exciting.

Q: Isn't it all right to believe we're doing the best we can only most of the time?

A: No, as that's like accepting the baby only if his diapers are clean. It's the whole package we want acceptance for, and that's what's so hard to give. Laying our non-acceptance on others is the way we hurt them, and all we do is get the worst out of them.

Q: What do you do when someone is expressing anger at you?

A: I breathe deeply and remember that I'm all right. (Remember the "bad guy" doesn't live with me anymore.) So I just listen and stay out of the way. I know the other wants to get through, as maybe he or she is saying, "I'm desperate ... no one really hears me ..." I'd say absolutely nothing while the anger is high and maybe not for some time later. Because I've listened so closely, whatever response I'll make will come after making the best possible observations of the entire situation.

Q: What's the difference between the other books, "Break the Anger Trap" and "The Anger Puzzle" ... and now this one?

A: Naturally Pat and I think this one is best. There's some overlap in all three books, but each one hits the subject from a different angle. It's my guess that you'll find plenty in the others to compensate for the overlap.

Q: Why do you think society made such a wrong turn and became obsessed with how we get anger out instead of looking at the way it's formed?

A: We've obviously known for a long time that talking had **some** connection with feeling better after getting angry. But instead of recognizing that it probably was the getting through (maybe later to a sympathetic third person) which was soothing to ruffled feathers, it was easy to jump to the conclusion that relieving the tension temporarily was all that was needed.

It's as if we thought that anger was hot air which needed releasing, and some counselors still goad their clients into getting their anger out. (Particularly for depressed people, this appears to bring them back to life, at least temporarily, and I know many counselors believe that it's impossible to be depressed and angry at the same time. See pages 89-90 and also "The Anger Puzzle," page 89, for my comments on this.)

In a counseling session I listen to **whatever** my clients want to say, and no time is spent specifically getting anger out. Why? I've learned that **when clients learn to stop forming anger today, their problems with anger disappear. Old buried anger is no longer a problem.** (The mindset which instantly "justified" anger is broken.)

So it's true that talking is related to easing anger. But from the way I see the entire picture, it's learning to talk more effectively which makes anger (and venting it) unnecessary.

Q: What's the best thing for you personally about being mostly without anger?

A: It's that people are willing to come close, and I'm getting tremendous amounts of information in addition to the good feelings which come with closeness. I love that. Before I became aware of all this, I kept seeing that people were backing away from me, yet it was so subtle that I couldn't put my hand on what was wrong. This kept the old bad-guy-something's-wrong-with-me feelings close to the surface.

Now I've listened long enough (and evidently made good enough observations) that I've found out how to live **my own life** enjoyably. You can probably imagine my pleasure to find that not only does all this work for me, but according to the feedback Pat and I are getting, it works for countless others too. No wonder we're celebrating!

What's extremely interesting to me is that Pat and I have traveled two completely different paths. From childhood he believed that he could "make it" by being a pleaser (usually trying to please a strong woman), and I very early found that I couldn't please (so I became more independent in order to cover up the fact that I didn't know how to get cooperation).

How amazing that what makes life better for both of us is the same thing: daily practice in getting through (as often as possible) without anger. □

Supplement #2

Some suggestions for *getting through without anger* . . .

1. It's important to prepare ourselves **before** trying to get through to another to get a fair hearing. This means giving ourselves a "ten" rating (on a scale of 1 to 10, that's the top), and holding onto it.

2. Be aware that many people are naturally defensive (afraid of hearing something which might make them look bad in their own or others' eyes). Since it is to our advantage that others are willing to talk to us, we need to compensate for their defensiveness by showing appreciation by keen listening.

3. It's good to remind ourselves that others aren't **automatically obligated** to listen just because we want to talk. (Nor are they obligated to talk just because we want information . . . or we're bored.)

4. It helps to be aware that **every time** we talk we are breaking into another's train of thought. We need to have a sense that our tidbits are from the sidelines, as the others' **processing their own information** is the main event... **for them**.

5. Listening, even *overlistening*, comes ahead of trying to get through. We need to have some idea of what we're feeding into, what's going on with the other. (Usually, if we listen closely enough, we hear this message: "Appreciate me.")

6. When we care to hear another person's feelings, it helps if we respond to show we have truly heard. Maybe we can say, "Sounds like you're feeling scared." (Or, "hurt," or "desperate," whatever seems appropriate.) **Real hearing is a precious gift we can give each other.**

7. We are not ready to try to get through until we check with the other for willingness to listen. "I've got some ideas about this, but I need to know if this is a good time to put them out . . ." (Nothing is more futile than talking if another doesn't choose to hear: "You listen" . . . "Now you listen to me" . . . "No, no, **you** listen to **me**.")

8. It's easiest to tell others how we feel if we are clear ourselves. It also helps to be able to keep our balance if we are continually aware of our feelings. Maybe we can describe them to ourselves by starting with physical feelings, as this may lead to awareness of deeper feelings. "I'm tense in my shoulders . . . Maybe I'm pushing too hard . . . I'm scared, trying too hard . . . pushing . . . afraid I won't make it."

9. When practicing telling others our feelings, it helps to start with minor ones first: "I feel kind of uneasy tonight." Don't be surprised if the other wants to know why you feel as you do, or wants to help you change the feeling. But you don't have to get trapped into trying to explain while the other judges if your feelings are "right" for you or not. Your feelings are *always right for you.* You can simply say, "All I know is that's what I'm feeling now, and I just wanted to tell you about it."

10. To break a two-person communication jam, sometimes it helps to try long monologues. One person talks until he or she chooses to stop, while the other makes notes. Then each switches parts, going back and forth, always waiting for the other to make a complete statement and be ready to listen before switching.

11. To minimize defensiveness in the listener, it helps to speak for ourselves:

> "I realize doing things your way is important to you and I can't expect you to be different . . . But I wouldn't feel right about myself if I didn't try to tell you how I feel. You wouldn't know unless I tell you, so I'm trying . . . **for my own reasons.** I'm working on the problem and I'm not sure yet what I'm going to do. But I wanted to let you know what's going on with me."

12. Instead of trying to impress others with our brilliant conversation, I like to remember a Portuguese saying that I consider to be the ultimate compliment: **"I like myself when I'm with you."**

13. In writing long notes, in an effort to break a communication jam, here are two suggestions:

> • One person writes a note and the other responds in writing, back and forth. Maybe a notebook can be kept in a certain drawer where each can look for responses.

> • Both write long notes, separately, on the same subject, exchanging notes and going back and forth.

14. Persistence is probably the main key to getting through. If we aren't heaping blame on those who don't hear us, they may be the ones to coach us on how we might get through. I believe we need to practice getting through *every day.*

15. Here's my definition of a friend: One who cares enough to give us feedback in a way we can take.

16. *I suggest you ask questions very, very sparingly.* This last suggestion is so important (yet seems so little understood) that I'm going to devote extra space to it. (Some American Indians go so far as to say that if we have to ask questions we aren't ready to learn the answers.)

Of course our own questions probably seem harmless to us. But it's too easy to forget that most of us, to some degree, live with the perpetual fear of being caught off guard, maybe feeling inadequate, looking stupid... like a "bad guy."

In our society, whenever we're asked questions, in order to be a "good guy" we're expected to respond (and maybe even be clever or helpful). We're suddenly forced to stop our own train of thought (no matter how exciting it might have been to us) and get with another's.

Probably you've had the experience of listening to questions and muttering to yourself, "What are they driving at?" Or if you've tried to answer you might have gotten this response, "No, no, that's not what I mean... what I want to know is..."

> We'll say someone hastily asks you, "What'll I fix for dinner?" Maybe you'll give a stumbling response which will irritate the questioner (whose thinking has probably already covered numerous possibilities). Then you too might become irritated because you'd been asked the question in the first place.
>
> It's easy to see that the other person would have been much more considerate of you if he/she had either 1) not asked the question at all, or 2) at the very least, revealed more of their train of thought **before** asking you to jump on the train:
>
> "I'm trying to decide if I need to go to the store or not... or if I'll just fix _____ ... but that might take too long as Sally has to leave by 7 o'clock... so maybe I'd better..."

It's true that your hearing such a rambling statement might have been an unwelcome intrusion on your thoughts. But at least you'd have been spared the irritations which might have followed your stumbling response.

When times are good, avoiding such irritations (whether you're asking questions or trying to respond) might not seem too important. **But in times of stress, even one unneccessary irritation can be too much.**

To break a questioning habit, probably at first all you can do, **after** you've asked a question, is to think of a statement you might have made instead. I predict that you'll be amazed how soon you'll see results if **even occasionally** you'll remember to avoid asking a question. You'll probably find yourself getting **different** information, and more of it... and I suspect it will be much more valuable... because it's willingly given. □

Supplement #3

(The following is from **Marriage Insurance**, which is a series of communication exercises for two people to use together.)

A Road Map

I wrote this material originally to give to my own clients so we wouldn't have to spend counseling time with he-did-this's and she-did-that's. And it worked. Since the first client who read it described it as a "road map," that name has stuck.

You may wonder why it seems important to offer a description of a marriage going downhill. But then you remember that when you yourself get a chance to see a whole map spread out at once, you usually find routes you don't expect. The opposite, as you can guess, might be wandering around lost, yet not even knowing there's a map to check.

The Trip Down

The first sign "the honeymoon is over" occurs when partners notice that their needs aren't met as fully as they once were.

It seems natural, when needs aren't filled the way one expects, to blame the person not filling the needs: the partner, of course.

Blaming, even if unexpressed directly, probably causes the partner to be less able and willing to do the expected need-filling.

Anger, whether open or denied, usually covers the hurts at the increasingly unfilled needs.

A kind of low-key power struggle begins in which each, probably in an indirect way, **is trying to force the other to fill needs as before.** Who starts the process doesn't really matter.

The methods used in attempts to make things better often perpetuate problems instead of solving them.

> A wife may talk little to her husband because she wants to avoid arguments. Her husband, desperate for more commuication, shouts and storms (overdoing it, no doubt) to provoke responsiveness. The wife's attempt to prevent arguments makes her "tune him out," blocking communication. The behavior of both, in attempting to make things better, actually makes them worse.

When problems seem to resist solution, each naturally wants to try harder (and oftener) to make things better. But the trying usually means merely adding new twists to the same methods which are perpetuating the problems.

Discomfort increases as basic needs for respect, security and emotional support are threatened more often, due to the trying harder. And the added amounts of disappointment, hurt, anger and blaming further reduce accurate communication.

In the absence of accurate communication, unflattering interpretations of the other's behavior fill the vacuum.

A wife believes her husband's silence is punishment of her when actually the silence may be due to hurt over previous attempts to communicate.

Unflattering interpretations of behavior justify and intensify the blaming of the other. The downhill slide of repeating patterns becomes even harder to reverse.

Misinterpretations of behavior mean that even a spouse's desired behavior may not make things better (the damned-if-I-do, damned-if-I don't pattern).

A wife begs her husband to stay home. He feels trapped and leaves, feeling guilty. When he later wants the security of home and returns, his wife believes it's only out of guilt, and not because he wants to, so she makes their time together miserable. Naturally the husband feels insecure and inadequate as a wife-pleaser (when he's away or at home) and the wife feels rejected and insecure (also whether he's away or at home), so a repeat of the pattern is assured.

Unawareness of one's misinterpretations about the other means that correcting distortions is impossible. Why should partners ask, and really want an answer, to the question "What's going on with you?" when they already "know" the answer?

A wife with preschool children is home, feeling trapped each day. She describes her husband as perfectly happy. "Why shouldn't he be happy? He's got everything he wants, freedom to run around all the time."

Her husband, uncomfortable at home with his family, yet not wanting to be "out in the cold," is

completely miserable. He describes his wife:
"Oh, she's happy all right. She's got the kids
and the house."

With so many obstacles (increasing pain, fear, insecurity) to accurate perceptions, most ways of problem-solving available to others go unseen and untried.

A husband threatens to leave every time there's an argument, so the wife believes she'd better become more independent. Her husband sees her moves toward independence and feels their relationship is threatened so he tries to thwart her. Such thwarting makes her pursue her plan to become independent more intensely, which triggers more intense thwarting behavior.

(What's impossible for each partner to see, when the downhill slide has gained such momentum, is that each person triggers the other's behavior which perpetuates the pattern. It's nearly impossible, then, for them to assure each other that they want to continue the relationship, thereby easing the insecurity of each and reversing the pattern.)

Hopelessness becomes a heavy burden as the weight of the downhill slide makes it appear that partners have tried everything, and nothing is ever going to work. As long as the primary goal of each is to force a partner to become a better need-filler, the power struggle can never end.

But the power struggle will give way at some point to a **goal of personal survival**, as partners eventually find they must put all of their energy into trying to feel good enough about themselves in order to be able to cope with

168

minimum requirements of survival. Any need-filling requests by the other, at this point, appear to be giant-sized, intolerable burdens. (This is usually the stage when one or the other moves out. Also suicide attempts or serious accidents sometimes occur at this point, as one partner makes a final desperate attempt to force the other to fill his/her needs.)

Survival behavior in one's self, naturally seems different from that of the spouse (who, in the other's mind, at least, is really mostly happy). When one is asking shrilly, out of pain and anger, "Why did you do this to me?," the answer, "I did it simply to survive," can't even be uttered, much less heard.

During this phase, one person may be feeling that he/she is totally wrong and the other totally right. (Others often reinforce this view. The partner who cares for small children is usually seen as good, for example, and anyone can tell that the spouse "out running around" is bad.) If a spouse accepts an angry partner's evaluation of him/her as a total failure as a need-filler, hence a failure as a person, there would be the possibility of suicide. No one can carry such total guilt for long: "I'm responsible for all our misery, and if I could just be different, everything would be all right." But with "being different" his/her only hope, and promises to "be good" nearly impossible to keep without awareness of the pattern the two of them are in, he/she is at a dead-end.

To resume pursuing even minimal survival activities, both must eventually conclude that he/she is mostly good, and it must be the partner who's bad. Unbearable fear that the opposite may be true must be squelched, maybe by anger.

Numbness may have taken over long before this point as a way of getting relief from too much hurt. But lessening one's sensitivity is self-defeating as it makes giving and receiving accurate information even more difficult.

Out of feelings such as numbness, helplessness and hopelessness, partners may strike out, possibly blindly, in attempts to feel better about themselves by demonstrating a capacity for violence or seeking other partners. But negative feelings, such as guilt and rejection, can hardly be avoided.

When partners discover that with a new person they can feel a little better about themselves, they often feel strong enough (and less forced to spend so much of their energy on survival) that they can try again with the original partner.

But confusion occurs at reconciliation attempts as the old, repeating patterns resist good-intentioned tampering. A dead-end is reached when each finally accepts the fact that he/she has no possible power to change the other, yet the bad partner, the one who obviously must change in order to make things better, simply isn't ever going to change.

Counseling? "I want to go but my partner doesn't." The underlying message still is, "I'm good, and he/she's bad. He/she, the villain, isn't even willing to try." The partner's unspoken response is probably, "It would only take one more failure to put me under for good, and I'm just not going to risk it."

The final, "this time for good" break-up occurs when at least one partner simply can't feel good enough about him/herself in the relationship any longer. The ratio of bad feelings to good has finally become completely intolerable.

The Turn-Around and The Road Uphill

Finding an uphill path won't occur until partners are far enough beyond the survival stage that they don't spend all their energy defending themselves and blaming the other. Because they aren't in as much pain, and therefore so intensely afraid of hearing even a hint of criticism, they can begin to hear others again. In this stage of openness, they may be able to learn from a marriage counselor, or by reading, or even listening a little differently to their same friends.

Progress occurs when partners can begin to hear each other's feelings more deeply. All each may hear at first is a little of the other's pain and survival struggle. But since each can identify with the same feelings, a bond flickers between them.

From that faint flicker, partners can begin to perceive each other a little more accurately. They then find it easier to accept the limitedness of the other's need-filling ability. **This acceptance alone eliminates a major source of anger and blaming, and of course the reactions to such anger and blaming.**

After a little time (with more hope present all the way) each can hear the other's expressions of feelings oftener, and each can make responses to show such hearing. Just one time when a formerly habitually-angry spouse listens sympathetically and says, "Sounds like you're really feeling hurt (sad, scared, or whatever is appropriate)," the other will probably feel a surge of joy and even more hope.

When the climate is established in which each really cares, even occasionally, to hear the other deeply (and neither rushes in to try to change the other's feelings), both experience the excitement of increased hope.

At some point each person realizes he/she must accept responsibility for taking the initiative for feeling good and getting his/her own needs filled. This means that for both, long-carried burdens, the assumed responsibilities for the other's needs and feelings, are lifted. And each, even halfway, no longer needs to accept blame for not perceiving and filling the other's needs.

When partners have less need to be defensive (they're not feeling blamed, inadequate and insecure), they can hear more and more. And each can see more clearly his own part in any interchange, especially how his/her own responses perpetuate, or end, a circular pattern. (He/she can choose, for example, to nourish security in his/her partner rather than insecurity.)

When both feel better about themselves, at least part of the time, they are able to willingly give their partners emotional support. (This is, of course, the same emotional support each was formerly trying to force from the other.)

The basic communication needed for day-to-day problem-solving, so difficult during the downhill spin, is at least possible now. Each has the skills to know how to get the best, instead of the worst, from the other.

There's no more helplessness, only choices of whether or not to use new skills.

True marriage insurance is a feeling, the feeling that exists when each gives the other deep respect, the kind that becomes emotional support. Then each can say to the other, "I feel good about **myself** when we're together." Protected by the comfort and security of such insurance, each can probably look back and see clearly: Greediness and manipulations to get more from a partner than he/she is willing or able to give, followed by disappointment and lack of acceptance of him/her as a need-filler, lead to marriage instability. But cultivation and maintenance of communication skills, which lead to respect for a partner and his/her feelings (emotional support), develops true marriage insurance, the kind that can withstand maximum stress. □

Supplement #4

Comments on angry pleasers (those whose lives are controlled by fear of others' anger)...

What I've written here is a detailed description of the way a compulsive pleaser gets trapped in an increasingly painful lifestyle. (I'm following the principle that the more accurately a problem can be described, the more likely it can be eased.)

The term "angry pleaser" is used because it's my observation that angry people are those who continue to believe they ought to be able to please others and avoid any possible anger; then they get angry and blame themselves (or others) for their inevitable failures; and in the increasing pain of an angry lifestyle, they stay trapped by their inability to see that it's the way they're defining problems which keeps them insoluable.

I What's Wrong

If you're a compulsive pleaser you're angry much of the time...

And you never can quite understand why your attempts to please don't get the results you expect.

> *"What's wrong?... What's wrong?... I was just trying to help... Why is everybody always jumping down my throat?"*

In your constant search to understand how to make things better, you're testing first one theory and then another: *"If only somebody would do this... or if only I could do that... or if only... if only... if only..."*

But your best theories never quite get you what you expect. And you really don't think you want too much: Just a little cooperation, even occasionally, or at least a tiny bit of appreciation... *"Nobody knows how hard I try."*

But you can't figure out what you're doing wrong. Surely you've got the power to make things better, haven't you? You'll just have to try harder... and harder... and harder...

II Something's Wrong with Me

Because you so often fail at getting what you want (respect, understanding, cooperation) you become increasingly afraid there's something wrong with you, something missing inside you.

Believing this helps you understand why you keep getting criticism for your best efforts.

In whatever way you define what's missing inside you, you ought to be able to figure out how to fill that empty space, shouldn't you? And then you could correct what's wrong, couldn't you?

Surely someday you'll be able to measure up, be where you want to be, "up to snuff." But it's not easy to fight something so vague. All you know for sure is that **it feels like there's a gap between where you are now and where you think you ought to be**.

This is so scary you need to prove to yourself (and everybody else if possible) that there's nothing wrong with you. You'll have to show you're above reproach, actually one of the good guys of the world.

The surest way to look good (to yourself at least) is to find opportunities for good deeds. Your helpfulness always gives you relief (if only temporary) from your fears of badness (inadequacy, being a nobody, or maybe just falling apart because of that missing space inside you).

It doesn't matter too much that your offering to help others may be irritating to them (as you're often implying that they can't do things right, your way). *"Here, use this knife to slice the tomatoes... it's better than that one..."*

What matters far more to you is that you can feel secure in the belief that you're being helpful. You live by the theory that if you do enough good deeds you'll feel better about yourself, and others will see your true worth. You've believed this for so long it never occurs to you to test the theory. But then it's never needed testing. It's been too easy to explain each failure: *"If I'd just tried harder (been good enough) I'd have made it."*

Feeling helpless would be intolerable. You can't consider the possibility that you might be incapable of making things better... someday.

But believing you continually need to try harder means that you can't slow down, whether in sickness or in health. You might "lose ground," or "lose your grip." Then your painful feelings of emptiness might rush out and overwhelm you.

So you keep moving faster and faster, hanging even more tightly to the hope that things will have to get better... if you'll just try hard enough. But things aren't getting better, and you're repeatedly left with the only conclusion which makes sense to you: *"There's got to be something wrong with me."*

III   The Search for Assurance

To continue to believe you have the power to make things better for yourself, you search even more diligently for proof of others' appreciation, acceptance, caring, cooperation, understanding...

You're busy evaluating what you're getting ("taking things personally"), and you can't seem to get quite enough of what you seek. *"Yes, they care for me, all right, but if they cared **enough**, they would..."*

175

Your constant search for that last drop of appreciation is risky because you're reading an evaluation of yourself into everything that happens: *"Am I getting what I deserve for what I do?"* Each time your answer is "no" you conclude you ought to be hurt. Then all your questions which follow lead nowhere: *"Am I really that bad?... Why do they do this to me?"*

Actually there's no way you can miss finding rejection as it's always out there, somewhere. Because your style is to "take things personally," finding any rejection at all is too much for you. You feel fragile, anyway, as if you're a house built of cards. It takes just removing one card (feeling one rejection) to bring the whole house crashing down.

> *"I was in the supermarket and I saw my best friend come in. And she actually turned the other way instead of coming over to talk to me as she usually does. It just kills me to have her treat me this way. All week I've gone over everything that happened when we were together last, and I just can't understand it. There's no reason for her to treat me like that." (Fact: The friend was having problems at home and was frantically trying to decide what to do. The last thing she could handle, just then, would have been trying to explain to someone else something she hadn't sorted out herself.)*

You continue to feel the rejection you despise so much because even those closest to you can't "bend over backwards" **enough**, or "go out of their way" **enough** so you can feel appreciated **enough**. (Because the first priority of all of us is keeping our own balance, in our own way, no matter how strange it may look to others, we're all extremely limited in how much we can help each other.)

But you're hurting (from the rejections) so you're searching harder and harder for evidence of appreciation in order to ease your hurts. Even though you believe you're hiding your disappointment in others (who aren't appreciating you enough) they most likely perceive it. **And they tend to feel inadequate around you, maybe guilty that they don't have**

more to give, or maybe resentful that they "owe" you for doing things they never asked you to do.

So what do they do? They get away if they can and try to find some place where they can feel better about themselves.

You're left confused and alone, repeatedly asking yourself the same questions.

> *"After all I've done for them, why are they leaving me?*
>
> *"What am I doing wrong? Don't they care they're making my life harder?*
>
> *"I never try to hurt anyone, why do they do this to me?*
>
> *"I want them to care enough to want to help me... why can't they do something for me just because they want to?"*

You search harder than ever for evidence that you're all right. Your only real comfort is the hope that you're capable of understanding what's going on... someday.

But sometimes you get so scared. What if the day is coming when you've tried everything you can think of? What if you really will be in a blind alley someday with nowhere to turn? **What if you never figure out how to be happy?**

All you know is that you can't stop trying to make things better. You can't take time out to lick your wounds. You absolutely have to search even more diligently for something else to try. Yes, someday, you'll find respect, closeness... happiness.

IV Who's to Blame

It seems as if you could get relief from your increasing pain if you could just know (for sure) who or what to blame. Then surely you'd know (for sure) what you ought to be trying next.

To cope with your ever-present fear that you're not good enough, coupled always with your desperate need to believe the opposite, you're diligent in finding evidence so you can justify blaming others for your troubles. And you don't mind looking to the past, present and future.

Armed with plenty of evidence of others' badness, you can keep letting them know how wrong they are so they'll change and things can get better for you. (Then you'll feel powerful, able to make things better, not helpless after all.)

You'll do whatever you need to do (and think whatever you need to think) as long as you can shift the blame away from yourself.

At least you can't feel helpless (or worthless). You can keep busy letting others know, maybe more and more forcefully, what you think they ought to be doing. Then they'll have to see things your way.

But it's hard to keep believing you're making things better when you're constantly triggering retaliation.

Because others don't enjoy assuming the position of villains around you **(just because they aren't doing what you think they ought to be doing so you can feel better about yourself)** they're confused and unhappy. And usually they're willing to let you know it.

Retaliation can be dangerous for many reasons, but the worst for you is that **it triggers your most painful fear: that maybe it really is your own badness that's the problem.**

Yet, as with any kind of blaming, it doesn't solve problems. **But you have to keep trying to make things better, don't you? If you quit trying you might as well be dead.**

Whenever the thought tries to surface that you yourself might be to blame, you have to dismiss it. The terror is too great to bear that you might not be doing the right things... **when you're trying night and day to find out what the right things are.**

In order to avoid such terror you have to focus **nearly every second** on trying to convince yourself and others that they are the ones causing your problems.

But you pay a heavy price for this lifestyle, as it means going around in circles. Your blaming others leads to their retaliation... to more blaming... to more retaliation...

V   Being Nice Is Better Than Getting Angry

But how can you get cooperation? How can you get help when you need it? How can you get others to stay close by? How can you feel better? **Will you ever be happy?**

You know you'd rather be nice than angry. You like it when others smile at you and want to be close, as then maybe you'll get some cooperation and your life will be easier.

But even when you try so hard to be nice, sometimes your anger comes out against your will. If you feel wronged enough, you may explode: *"You're a stupid jerk... it's your fault that things are all messed up... I'm sick and tired of what you're doing..."*

Although you'd like to believe things will get better after your outburst, they actually get worse. Those you've yelled at may conclude that you're the one who's the jerk. **And you probably triggered their own guilt, their fears of being bad, wrong. So they either want to fight you... or stay away.**

But you have to believe that any time you get angry it must be others' fault. *"If only they'd do what I want, I wouldn't have to scream at them... (and then I could be nice, the way I'm trying to be...)."*

Whenever your anger breaks loose (and shocks you as much as others) it doesn't mean you've lost faith in the power of your niceness. **No one regrets that you lost your temper any more than you (contrary to what bystanders may think).**

Each time you get angry, it's because you feel helpless and desperately disappointed that the power of your niceness isn't enough to get what you want.

But you know your anger pushes others away. So what can you do? **Be nicer, of course.** You find yourself continually making vows to try harder to be nice. Surely, **if you try hard enough**, you can keep from blowing up and ruining everything.

But it's confusing when sometimes your anger comes out and it feels good. You get a burst of relief from physical tension and also a surge of power (even if brief). That power is especially welcome because it banishes fears of your helplessness.

You want very much to believe that your anger will get you what you want... once and for all, and then you won't have to get angry again. But your anger never gets you what you expect... once and for all... **even when others meet your demands.**

> *"My guitar was destroyed in a house fire and all I could do was complain to my partner. Every day, complain, complain. So he finally went out and bought me a new guitar, but he spent more than we could afford. So I felt guilty, then worse and worse. It got so bad I couldn't enjoy playing the guitar at all. (But things got worse when my partner got mad at me. He took it as a personal insult that I didn't appreciate his gift.)"*

For one thing, when you're controlling others with your anger, you can't ever tell whether they're doing what you want because they care for you... or because they fear your anger.

And no matter how another responds to your anger, you can't really know the damage you do.

But one reason your outburst doesn't get what you want is that you may feel so embarrassed and ashamed of your anger (in such a nice guy as you) that you apologize immediately. *("I didn't mean it... I'm just having a bad day...")* Then you've nullified any chance of getting even temporary changes from others (even if grudgingly given).

But what's worse is that you know from experience that your anger hurts you, especially in the long run. Yet you keep finding yourself angry, again and again. And you know you're building higher hurdles between you and your real goals (closeness, cooperation, caring...).

Whenever you "tell off" others you get a predictable result:

> Either you reap instant rebellion (even if silent) and more resistance to the changes you've been seeking by your niceness...

> Or you get instant compliance (from another pleaser). Since in the long run such pleasers will pull away from you, your "telling off" another isn't helping you at all, unless your goal is to be isolated.

You hate so much to be isolated by your anger you continue to believe you have just one choice: be nicer.

VI   The Need to Avoid Feedback

Because you already hurt so much (at failing to get what you want either by your niceness or anger) you have to avoid feedback at all costs. (You never know in advance what you'll hear, and there's always criticism lurking out there, somewhere, ready to disgrace you in an unguarded moment.)

So you find yourself incessantly defending your helping/pleasing lifestyle to yourself and to others. **You'll tell yourself whatever is necessary to stay convinced that such a lifestyle is working for you.**

You're becoming so vigilant in detecting possible criticism that every move you make is controlled by the need to avoid seeing even minor hints of others' disapproval.

But blocking feedback in order to avoid criticism means that you're trying to make things better without getting accurate information about what's going on around you.

Instead of making your life easier, it's the opposite. All your problem-solving is confused when it's based on your guesses about what's going on... and what you think ought to be going on.

You're becoming trapped inside your own head, left mostly with your own observations and your own ways of processing information. **This is a dangerous price to pay for your safety from criticism.**

Yet even in isolation it isn't always possible to believe that it's others who are causing your problems. The fear that you yourself might be bad is always just under the surface. What if you really aren't capable of making it?

Even asking the question causes terror, terror so great it propels you to break isolation and risk getting feedback once again. Surely you can show others how valuable you are and then you'll get the appreciation you deserve. *"Just tell me what I'm doing wrong and I'll correct it."*

But fresh from your isolation, you aren't able to see problems clearly and define them accurately. So it's inevitable that the ways you're choosing to make things better usually make them worse instead. The more you think you win, the more you actually lose. **You're in a pattern of trying harder and enjoying it less.**

Maybe you put all your energy on appearances, for example, so no one will suspect there's something wrong with you. *"If I can just look good enough, I'll be all right."* But the contrast between how you look to others, and what you feel inside, gives you one more reason to feel bad. **It's as if you're not only feeling empty, wrong, inadequate, but you're also a fraud, hiding the truth from others.** So the more you believe you succeed at looking good, the greater is your pain because others don't know how to relate to you. Because they may perceive you as "having it all together," they don't believe you when you try to tell them it isn't true.

You may have a passion for order, whether in material things or people. It's terribly important to you that others see you as knowing how things ought to be. But this is exhausting for you and irritating to others. They continually resist your attempts to get them to help you keep everything and everybody shaped up. So the harder you try to make things better, the more you get the opposite.

Maybe you exaggerate your achievements in your desperate need to feel important. But others may not respond with compassion because they may not realize you're trying to compensate for your fears of failure. **So they get irritated at your exaggerations and ignore you, and you feel less important than ever.**

Maybe you give presents you can't afford. But whenever you give to others out of your own need to be seen as a good guy, it's not surprising that the responses to your giving may be disappointing.

It's possible you believe the real cure for your troubles would be to find a partner who would appreciate you properly. So maybe you spend your energy searching repeatedly and in vain for that partner. But you'll probably intensify your niceness in an effort to hold onto a prospective partner, always expecting that your niceness can get that continuous stream of appreciation you crave.

But the prospective partners fear you'll expect more in return for such niceness than they can give. **So they pull away from you rather than stay and feel inadequate, never able to give you enough.**

You probably are constantly criticizing just about everything in an effort to raise yourself up a little. But those around you become uneasy when they wonder what you say about them behind their backs.

You constantly return for comfort to your all-time favorite way of showing you're above reproach (and can't possibly deserve anyone's anger, criticism, blaming). You can always do another good deed. Then it won't matter what's going on around you, as at least briefly you can convince yourself that you're more than just all right, you're actually a good guy. But when you do good deeds out of your need to be recognized and have impact, you may be overdoing it. **Then others may be forced to reject you in order to be safe from your interference in their lives.**

You've long believed that you have the power to know what others want... and that you're able to give it to them. **But to continue to believe this you have to be sure you hide the evidence of your failures... especially from yourself.**

So you're working every second at justifying your lifestyle to yourself, and you succeed, sometimes, at least from your own point of view. But being locked into the need for holding onto this safe point of view creates more problems. Others' feedback to you isn't making sense. You constantly find yourself saying, *"I can't understand... there's no reason for that... why?... why?... why?..."*

Any time there's a conflict between what another person says and your perceptions, you have to work hard to preserve your own version of the truth.

Other people may be trying in vain to get through to you, to help you understand why your lifestyle is hurting you so much. But sometimes, because they don't want to hurt you, they have trouble telling you the truth. For example, they probably don't want to say, *"You're driving me crazy when you do that."* Instead they might say, *"Don't bother."* And maybe you'll respond, *"Oh, it's no bother."* Then you continue to do what the other didn't want you to do in the first place.

But when others repeatedly can't get through to you in serious matters so you'll at least listen to their views, you're in real danger. It's when others become desperate enough in their failure to get through to someone that they may resort to violence.

But your lifestyle depends on staying inside your own world with your own point of view. That's the only way you can be safe and continue to believe that you truly are helping others. **But you have to repeatedly explain to yourself that it's only because others are ungrateful that you don't get the rewards you deserve.** Otherwise you'd have no explanation as to why others seem to be making your life harder.

But you're seriously handicapped in day-to-day problem-solving. **You're trapped between the necessity for corrective feedback (to assure your own safety and survival) and the fear of getting it.**

VII   The Truth Gets Lost... Sometimes

You search to understand what's wrong (so you can make things better) but you're floundering because you can't get accurate feedback. But how can you get feedback when you're afraid of it? How can you know your effect on others? How can you know if you're expecting too much of yourself or others?

It's practically impossible for you to tell others the truth as you're so afraid of criticism: *"Oh no, let me do it... No, I don't mind... You go off and enjoy yourself."* You'll say nearly anything to avoid **even the possibility** of another's showing disappointment or irritation.

Maybe you tell yourself you can't tell the truth because you don't want to hurt anyone. But what you're probably doing is trying to avoid **seeing** any hurt feelings in another's eyes (**as that would be proof to you that you're really a bad guy in disguise**). *"I'd rather run and hide than see her cry. So I just say what I think she wants to hear... or else I avoid talking to her at all."*

Because you know that you're sometimes unable to tell the truth, you suspect that others may be the same way. And this realization makes you increasingly uncomfortable. How can you get along in a scary world if you can't tell what's going on?

Maybe you'll never find out how to be happy, and you'll just be miserable the rest of your life.

This thought is so frightening you've got to work harder to understand what's going on. But you may be getting the truth from others (especially pleasers) only when they're angry, after their nice-guy act has fallen apart. By then their feedback is just too harsh and you have to push it away. *"They're just mad because I'm not doing more... they never liked me anyway... they take me for granted, that's why they act like they don't appreciate what I do."*

It also makes it hard for you to understand what's going on when others are so embarrassed about their anger they instantly apologize. *"I didn't mean it... you know that..."*

Because you want so badly to believe they didn't mean it, that's what you choose to believe... to your own confusion.

The belief isn't comfortable as it conflicts too much with your own evidence. **You know that when you yourself are angry, you do mean what you say, at least for that minute.** Of course you may feel different later and regret what you said.

Even if you're uncomfortable in believing that others don't mean what they say in anger, you're forced to believe it. It's a necessity if you're to feel safe from your too-painful fears of badness.

Because your entire life is a struggle to understand what's going on so you can avoid others' anger, you feel you have no choice but to be nicer... and nicer... and nicer.

So you continue trying to read minds in order to give others what you think they want. But you're continually surprised and hurt that you're getting so much criticism for your best efforts.

Even if it were possible for others to tell you what they want, and if it were possible for you to deliver it exactly, they still might blame you if they're not pleased. Your failure, in their eyes, would be that you didn't make them feel as good as they expected.

It's becoming increasingly evident that a lifestyle of trying to please others (so you can believe you're making them happy and you can feel like a good guy) keeps you in an impossible position. **It guarantees that much of the time you'll be failing and frantically trying to find out what's wrong. And to you, this means finding who or what to blame.**

But your blaming (whether it's self-anger or anger directed at others) keeps you caught in a circular trap of hurting more, trying more and failing more... then hurting/trying/failing... And you're no closer to understanding what's wrong or how to make things better.

When you find yourself overcommitted you can hardly face letting someone down (who might then think you're bad). So you may try to borrow strength from others: *"Will you stop by Joe's house... somebody's got to help him..."*

Because others resist your including them in your helping-pleasing lifestyle, they may get angry at you. But you get angry at them in return, as they're depriving you of the chance to be an even better guy (stronger and more powerful).

How can you ever get enough strength to make it when others won't help you? It isn't easy when others are hearing this confusing message: *"I'm so overwhelmed, nobody understands how hard I try... But let me do it all... I'm so eager to look like a good guy (and get a drop of appreciation) that I welcome the opportunity to do more."*

No wonder others pull away in confusion and you're continually discouraged. But you're not a quitter. So you push on, telling all who will listen, *"Here, let me help."* But all the while your self-doubts come through, *"What if I'm doing everything wrong?"*

Most of your energy is going to guard the dark secret that you really are a bad guy because of all the stupid things you do. How can you live with the risk of exposing that bad guy hidden in there? It's like knowing there's a monster inside, always ready to jump out and embarrass you.

Because you can't admit your failures, limitations, errors or misjudgments (even to yourself) you're seriously handicapped in the way you relate to others. How can they know what's going on with you if you can't tell them?

Even when others treat you well or give you a compliment, you feel guilty and can't accept it. *"They just don't know what I'm really like."*

Others are increasingly uncomfortable with you because what you're saying isn't quite adding up.

VIII   Nothing is Better

Those around you seem to be expecting you to do more and more and more. Because they may see you as strong (as you try so hard to show you are), they may be saying, *"Oh, let him/her do it... He/she likes to do everything..."*

Your confusing messages mean that your fantasy of getting help, of being rescued from your overcommitments, continues to be only a fantasy. **No matter how much you try to get help, you can't find enough to make you feel good.**

When bystanders see that you're exhausted and over-extended, they can't understand why you don't take their advice: *"You've got to stand up for yourself and say 'no' more often."* What they don't see is that you're incessantly looking for opportunities to do good deeds... for your own reasons (in order to avoid feeling like a bad guy).

So your short-term success is doing the deed... even if you have to ignore the response you get (maybe from both the recipient of the deed as well as bystanders).

One reason you hate to say "no" is that you identify with others who are hurting... all the time, as you're imagining that you understand how they feel. You long to ease their burdens. You know how much you yourself desperately crave help sometimes.

So you're constantly thinking of others. You want to be ready to help them, even if only to give good advice.

But you take it personally if the help/advice isn't taken. **It's as if each rejection means a step backward for you, just one more blow falling on your already-bruised head.**

You hate to say "no" to anyone asking for help. And when you do say "no" (and feel guilty), you blame the person who asked for help because you're feeling guilty.

In your confusion and pain, all you know for sure is that something is terribly, terribly wrong. And you feel like a failure more and more often.

No matter what the facts of any situation, you're probably muttering on and on and on: **"I couldn't let him fall on his face, could I?... I didn't want to see her disappointed... I didn't have any choice... I had to... She needs me... I was so tired I could hardly move..."**

You often feel that you're out of control, careening between one good deed and another. And you feel "caught in the middle" at times as you can't continually please two different people (and avoid their anger). But you have to believe it's their fault you're "caught in the middle."

Maybe you're following in the unhappy footsteps of someone you knew in childhood who would complain bitterly, *"You ungrateful wretches... I'm working my fingers to the bone for you... and the only reward I'll ever get will be in heaven."*

You're increasingly confused by the way others react to your blaming them for not helping you (to do what you're choosing to do). You have trouble understanding why they seem to blame you for everything that's wrong.

Since you've believed so long that **you** have the power to make others feel good (by your helping/pleasing) it's no wonder that **they too** expect you to make them happy. And if they aren't as happy as they think they ought to be, you tell yourself that it's your fault. **It's always easy to believe that you just aren't doing all you ought to be doing.**

IX Futile Power Struggles

But the tragedy of your lifestyle (of trying so hard to convince yourself you're good enough) is that it appears to others that you're always trying to be one-up, better than those around you.

This has a serious, unwanted side effect: Others believe you're seeing them as one-down and they don't like it. So they look for opportunities to "cut you down to size."

The problem comes from your belief that you can't just do what others do and feel good about yourself. For you it takes doing more, as you're trying to fill that missing space inside you, be "up to snuff" as you believe you ought to be.

Because others continually see you straining, striving and pushing, when they're around you they're conscious of feeling either up or down.

But the real problem is that it's unlikely you're aware of playing one-up, yet that's what makes others defensive around you. Because you're unaware of the cause of the damage you're doing, you're unable to correct it.

In your habitually helpful style you might be continually saying such things as this: *"Here, do it this way. Let me show you."* Often others see you as if you're assuming that you're the standard of the way things ought to be. *"I do this... you should too."*

Yet from your point of view you're only trying to get others (and yourself) to see how valuable you are.

But what's happening is that in your need to continually justify your lifestyle you don't realize how such justifications are sounding to others. What they hear is this: *"I'm always right... better than those around me."*

Your confusion is real when you get a glimpse of what others are thinking: *"Oh, he thinks he's perfect."* **Since you don't feel perfect... at all, you don't understand the criticism... at all.**

Others may perceive you as strong and independent, never suspecting that this is a pose you've forced yourself to accept... all because you've never been able to figure out how to get cooperation.

It's true, however, that sometimes the worse those around you look, the better you feel: *"At least I'm not doing that... and that... and that..."* But you have mixed feelings. You continually tell yourself that if others aren't happy around you it must be a reflection on you. So you vow to do the right things more and more often.

What you're missing, to your constant peril, is the awareness that you're in a world in which others also want to feel good about themselves. And they want to do it just as you do, by showing how capable they are. (The reason this is so hard for you to see is that when you take over, others probably back away.)

You're seriously handicapped in the way you relate to others when it's essential to you that you keep the one-up spot (even if you don't realize that's what you're doing). The only people who can be comfortable around you must be willing to play one-down. After so long, when they fully understand the role they are expected to play around you, they may either fight you for the one-up position... or they may get away (even if only mentally).

It's most likely that those around you at one time wanted nothing more than to please you. And as they leave, they probably are mumbling: *"I never could do enough..."*

In your incessant need to get assurance that you truly are all right, no one can give you enough appreciation. There isn't enough appreciation available, anywhere, to ease the pain of your helping/pleasing/one-up lifestyle.

When others try to explain how they feel around you, you still find it difficult to believe your overhelpfulness (over-niceness, over-protectiveness) is a put-down to them. But it's as if you're constantly saying to everyone who will listen:

> *"I can do that... you can't.*
> *"I'm strong... you're weak.*
> *"Let me do everything... you'll probably mess up.*
> *"I'm smart... you're stupid."*

Others may not realize how strongly you need to be constantly trying to help them (for your own reasons). **So they take your behavior to be an indication you continually see them as inadequate, bad, and just not what they ought to be.**

They feel guilty and confused. *"After all the help he/she's given me, why do I feel so terrible and always want to get away? I must really be the world's worst heel."*

It's difficult for you to see that your helpfulness is a constant put-down to others. So you continue to say to yourself, *"It surely can't be a crime to try to help, can it?"* **And you choose to believe it's virtuous to keep doing the same things.**

It would probably be inconceivable to you that just offering to help sometimes may be offensive, regardless of the facts of any situation. Your offer may just be an irritating reminder of your assumed one-up status, just one more of your continuing demonstrations that obviously you're in better shape than those around you, always able to lean over and help some peasant down below who just isn't up to your level.

Whatever is going on, you too find yourself defensive and confused: *"Since I was just trying to help, that can't possibly be bad. If you want to bite my head off, you must be the one who's bad."*

When two people are relating to each other in a one-up/one-down pattern, both usually can play both parts. But the one-down position is assumed unwillingly. So power struggles go on and on. *"I'm right, so obviously you must be wrong." "No, no, you're the one who's wrong..." "You're crazy"... "You're the one who's crazy..."*

Of course there's no winning. Even if the losers seem beaten down for good, they're really only biding their time, waiting for a chance to be one-up. It's a never-ending roller coaster, and no part of the ride feels good.

With two pleasers interacting (and all of us are pleasers to some extent) the possibilities for pain are endless. The more each person hurts, the more each person tends to play one-up (even if only mentally) in an attempt to feel better... and the more ugly the consequences.

In so much misery it's difficult for either of you to see how much you're alike. **You may be fooled by the fact that one of you is pushing, trying to make things better by doing more, and the other is withdrawing, trying to make things better by doing less.** Outsiders believe they know who is "right" or "wrong," but actually both of you are fighting to keep your balance in the only way you know. Look at the similarities:

Neither of you feel as good about yourselves as you think you ought to.

And both of you try desperately to avoid the other's anger.

So you both are afraid to really listen to the other, which means that neither of you feel you can get through to the other.

And both of you probably make things worse by blaming either yourself or the other.

Yet both of you are hungry for the same respect, appreciation, understanding, caring...

And both of you simply don't know how to get such good feelings.

Part of the time you both believe in the power of your niceness (as you know your anger doesn't work for you). But you get angry anyway, whether you believe you really ought to or because it comes out unbidden. But at times you hate yourself for being too nice.. and ineffective. *"I really ought to put my foot down."*

But you find, repeatedly, that when neither anger nor niceness gets you what you want, your confusion and pain and loneliness increase.

So you crave even more comfort, respect, understanding...

But you're feeling tremendously helpless most of the time, as such rewards seem constantly moving further out of your reach.

In your misery you each tend to see only your own pain. And you believe the other really ought to care enough to make your life easier. Both of you are saying to the other: *"You're not even trying to help me."*

X You Want Real Help

You know you long for help in finding a more comfortable lifestyle, but what kind of help do you need? and where to find it?

Your life becomes a search for the right kind of help, the kind which fits you, the kind which will lead to your getting cooperation, appreciation, happiness...

Even if you were able to know exactly the kind of help you wanted, it wouldn't be possible to find anyone willing and able to give it when and how you want it. Yet when others' help doesn't seem to help, your tendency is to conclude it must be your fault, somehow, some way.

Maybe this is like being lost in a wilderness, on a wrong path, but convinced that if you'll just stay on the path long enough and try harder (be nicer to everyone you meet) you'll reach your destination.

But so far you haven't been able to take others' suggestions for finding a better path. Just seeking advice is hard enough, but rejecting it is even more painful. You have to see others' disappointment in you (whenever they feel your rejection). So you're left feeling you must be worse than all others if you can't even take good advice (especially when it comes from someone who really cares for you, one who really wants to help you).

Sometimes you feel obligated to take advice even if you've tried it before and know it won't work. Because you're hurting so much yourself, and can't bear to see the hurt in another's eyes at your rejection, you take the advice anyway. Yet you know you'll be the loser, just chalking up one more failure.

Maybe it's too uncomfortable to talk to others about what's really going on with you. To ask for help you'd have to risk revealing your failures, your feeling of emptiness. Just being reminded of the deep gap between your good-guy appearance and what you really feel inside would mean abandoning your entire lifestyle (which has been based on avoiding seeing that gap).

But sometimes you do talk to others when you're secure in the belief that they can't possibly suspect there's anything wrong with you. But you have to be on guard to keep the conversation superficial so you can avoid serious feedback. You can't risk hearing anything from anyone who suspects what's really going on inside you.

Maybe at some point in your search for help you do find others who share similar experiences. Then you can talk and maybe listen, and at first it feels great to find out you're not alone. But you soon realize you may not be finding help in breaking the pattern you're in. Others may still be lost in the same wilderness.

It's possible you're one of those who can talk easily and incessantly about how wronged you've been, how bad others are and how helpless you are to make things better. Others probably pull away from you when they find there is no end to your story, just more details of the same plot.

Maybe you believe that getting your anger out will get rid of it. So you get it out. But the anger doesn't dissipate. In fact, telling others of your troubles may attract allies, and you'll reinforce each other. You may get even angrier at those villains you believe are doing you wrong. **Or you may get angrier at yourself and feel even more guilty and helpless because you aren't making things better.**

It may be a relief if others leave you alone. You can't stand to hear, one more time, *"You've got to take responsibility for yourself... You've got to..."* Little do others know how hard you try... and try... and try.

Your only conclusion is that no one can possibly understand you. You must be totally different, wrong, bad. You're left more and more alone with your pain, alone and lost in a wilderness.

XI   Time to Give Up?

At some point maybe you decide to quit trying so hard... then it won't hurt so much to fail. So you do nothing for awhile, just give up.

You've been increasingly isolated anyway, but now you're giving up your search for understanding. **If you'll just stumble along and make no decisions then maybe you'll be safe from criticism and pain.** Maybe you can just play "Follow the Leader."

But others criticize you for making no decisions, and this reinforces your self-hate because you've given up.

In your isolation, even if it's of your own choosing, your pain is so great that sometimes you feel an overwhelming urge to find proof you're not totally bad. But every time you come out of isolation, you return to the trap of the same hurt-try-fail cycle. So you give up once more.

You may try suicide, **or just feel miserable over a period of many, many years**. Maybe all that changes at different times is the degree of misery.

To others your behavior may seem bizarre, as maybe all they can see is your anger alternated with your niceness. **They know they can't feel safe from your anger... or help you feel better.**

In this state of misery you'll do anything (however ridiculous and obnoxious) to keep others from moving away from you. But they move away just the same. So you get angrier and maybe try to force them to stay close. Then, as they inevitably have to get away, there's no one to comfort you in your pain.

You're now totally alone to deal with the consequences of your behavior. At last you're totally convinced that you're really the worst of all bad guys.

Probably the easiest way to avoid your unbearable pain is to go numb, turn yourself off and feel nothing. **No good feelings can get through your numbness, however, so you're paying an enormous price to avoid bad feelings.**

It's a real handicap to try to function without being aware of your feelings. You take what people say literally, as if you have to stay on the surface of every conversation, not get down where feelings might burst out. So you aren't in tune with where most people live, which is with their feelings. It's as if you're always out of touch, on the sidelines, alienated, alone in a world of your own.

Your problems are increasing whenever you're so numb you can't be sensitive either to your own feelings... or others'. **You have to live by your guesses of what you think you feel... and also what you think others feel. You're living without the most valuable tool for running your life, genuine sensitivity.** Because you have long thought you understood others' feelings, you've believed you were unusually sensitive. The belief in your unusual sensitivity is probably the explanation you're giving yourself for being a helper/pleaser. But this is the kind of one-up belief (**that others are insensitive as compared to you**) which infuriates them. Yet you need to keep the belief in order to account for the fact that others don't see things your way.

Without genuine sensitivity to your own feelings, your decisions about what you ought to be doing are more than ever off target. Less often are others hesitating to say to you, *"You're driving me crazy."*

In your numbness you try in vain to find something which will excite you, wake you up, make you feel good. But when you're so numb, nothing feels good. You find yourself sadly saying, *"I don't know what I want."*

Others may persist: *"Get out of my hair. Go find something of your own to do."* But you can't without feeling guilty that you're letting everyone down by not putting your energy into helping them.

You may have all kinds of health problems as your body is telling you that you can't go on. Maybe you feel pain in your chest, for example, as if you're holding your breath, afraid to breathe for fear of hurting someone. You may be telling yourself, *"That's all bad guys can do, hurt the ones they love."*

Fortunately, every time you need to feel better, even if only briefly, you can find someone to blame. *"It's my bad partner. If I can just leave him (her) I'll be all right."*

Whenever you hurt more than you can stand, you'll try any form of painkiller (legal or illegal), whatever the consequences. Maybe you'll live inside a fog of daydreams, or go anywhere or do anything to escape the too-great misery of your down-to-earth activities.

But this makes every necessary down-to-earth activity more difficult. So both your real and perceived failures are multiplying.

When you've withdrawn far enough from your misery that you believe you can stay safe from criticism and rejection, **maybe your anger is the only feeling strong enough to cut through your numbness. So you get angry in order to feel alive, have impact, feel important. You tell others how bad they are for not doing what you think they ought to be doing. Your hope is always that if you can just get angry enough (or show how hurt you are) others will change so you can feel better.**

But as always, your anger pushes others further away. They don't care to hear you just so you can feel more alive, feel that you have impact, that you're really not on the sidelines.

Because you still believe in the power of being nice (if you could just do it) your getting angry (no matter how justified it seems) is painful evidence you're just not good enough, not nice enough. In fact, there's no longer any doubt: you really are a bad guy.

At times, you even feel you might as well act like one and let everyone know how bad you really are. It's almost a relief after trying so long to be nice.

At last your helplessness is total. No matter what you do, or how much you hurt, you can't find how to get others to come close and comfort you.

How is it possible to get off such a path? I'll summarize the way I see the problem and I think you'll clearly see how a solution emerges.

Angry pleasers are those who 1) perceive themselves as bad and live in fear of others' anger (which would

199

confirm their perceived badness); 2) so they reach the conclusion that they should spend all their energy proving that they're not bad after all; 3) but when they don't really believe that themselves, all their "proving" efforts are futile, and 4) in confusion and pain, they become stuck in compulsive behavior which not only is unrewarding to themselves but triggers anger in others; 5) so it seems that no matter what they do, they get the opposite of the closeness and comfort they want.

All it takes to get off the angry-pleaser path, the way I see it, is to realize that **we have a choice** about the way we see the world. If we want to, we can see a world in which **all of us** are doing the best we can, all the time, just trying to keep our balance. **Or we can choose to believe the opposite.**

I've tried to show in these pages the result of the latter choice.

Also, I thought you'd like to see, if you're an angry pleaser, that you weren't crazy for making the decisions you did. Each one seemed totally logical, based on your starting place of not feeling good about yourself.

What helps me choose to believe that I'm doing the best I can all the time, just trying to keep my balance in ways no one else can ever understand, is this: I can never know, for sure, what is right for me at any one minute **until I try it. This means I'm certain it's impossible for anyone else to know.**

If others want to pretend they know, and get angry with me, it's apparent to me their anger is their own thing (and they're whirling inside their own anger trap).

I don't have to pass out when I'm the target of anger, and I don't ever have to hang my head and apologize for my "badness".... or make everything worse **for myself** by returning anger.

When we're no longer controlled by fear of others' disapproval/disappointment/anger, we're free to be working at keeping our own balance. And from that position our choices become better and better.

Of course we'll continue to choose to try to help each other, occasionally, and even try to please each other, occasionally. But we can also see that **our most valuable helping probably is indirect, maybe completely unexpected... and probably unconsciously given and maybe unconsciously received.**

The more we feel good about ourselves, the less the old-angry pleaser lifestyle can creep back to control us. It's as if continual focusing on keeping our own balance makes everything and every decision seem new... and exciting.

If we think of a baby's trying to learn to walk from watching others, we can see what's happening. There's no way we can learn to keep our balance except by finding the courage to risk trying the first baby steps.

Yet it's a risk-taking which never stops. We can fail at any time and maybe feel foolish, exposed as a bad guy, incompetent, a disgrace.

But it's only by taking the risks inherent in balancing that we can move ahead. The opposite is to be afraid to move for fear of incurring even the faintest possibility of anger, then compounding our problems by blaming others because we ourselves are afraid to move.

When we're not incessantly and blindly trying to get others' goodwill, it's as if we can open our eyes and see a world in which all of us are engrossed in the same scary balancing act. There's no one-up or one-down, just people struggling in different places and in different ways.

I see all of us as making decisions by processing our lifelong collection of bits and pieces of information, trying to decide what our next step should be. **It's as if, minute by minute, we're sorting through our private "garbage" heap.** Many of the fragments are barely recognizable, although sometimes we might glimpse a priceless jewel. (We'd probably like to think of our minds as full of neat rows of orderly thoughts. But I'm using the term "garbage" to imply that much of what comes into the pile is in unrelated segments, and they certainly don't all come by our choice.)

However we describe our process of decision making, it's clear that no one else could ever have access to all the pieces of our garbage heap, much less could anyone else be able to determine what our next step should be... or how to take it. **So we're left essentially alone with the most important... and risky... job of our lives.**

And it's not easy to get much comfort from each other, as we can never explain what's going on with our garbage-sorting-decision-making at any one time. The accumulating garbage is shifting too fast, and we can't talk fast enough to keep up with our brain. And even if we could, others are limited in their willingness to drop their own garbage-sorting-balancing very often and listen to us.

Yet it's a real comfort when others try to hear what's behind our decisions. And it's especially comforting when they don't offer "help" and overload the shifting mass of garbage we're straining to sort out.

To me, what I believe keeps us from returning to our old lifestyle is gaining **firsthand** experience of the complexity and riskiness of **just keeping our own balance**.

It's this awareness which creates genuine compassion and appreciation for every other human being. And it's this same compassion and appreciation which makes it possible to feel the good feelings which come from listening deeply to each other... and responding deeply.

From this point on, everything we do, including the risk-taking we feared so much, is less hazardous. We're not alone and stuck, repeatedly asking, "What's the matter with me?" Instead, we're moving, living, and with eyes wide open. And it's exciting. □

BIBLIOGRAPHY

Adams, David, The Role of Anger in the Consciousness Development of Peace Activists: Where Psychology and History Intersect, *International Journal of Psychophysiology* 4, 157-164. 1986

Allman, W.F., A Laboratory of Human Conflict, *U.S. News & World Report*, April 11, 1988.

Beck, Aaron T., *Cognitive Therapy and the Emotional Disorder*. New York: International Universities Press, 1976.

Burns, David, *Feeling Good*, New York: Basic Books (Harper Colophon), 1973

Chesney, Margaret A., Roseman, Ray H., (Eds.), *Anger and Hostility in Cardiovascular and Behavioral Disorders*. Washington, D.C.: Hemisphere Publishing Corporation, 1985.

> Chesney, Margaret A., Anger and Hostility: Future Implications for Behavioral Medicine.

> Durel, Lynn A. and Krantz, David, The Possible Effects of Beta-Adrenergic Blocking Drugs on Behavioral and Psychological Concomitants of Anger.

> Gentry, W. Doyle, Relationship of Anger-Coping Styles and Blood Pressure among Black Americans.

> Hecker, Michael H.L. and Lunde, Donald T., On the Diagnosis and Treatment of Chronically Hostile Individuals.

> Julius, Stevo, Schneider, Robert and Egan, Brent, Suppressed Anger in Hypertension: Facts and Problems.

> Manuck, Stephen B., Kaplan, Jay R., and Clarkson, Thomas B., An Animal Model of Coronary-Prone Behavior.

> Megaree, Edwin I., The Dynamics of Aggression and Their Application to Cardiovascular Disorders.

BIBLIOGRAPHY

Navaco, Raymond W., Anger and Its Therapeutic Relation.

Patterson, G.R., A Microsocial Analysis of Anger and Irritable Behavior.

Reid, John B. and Kavanagh, Kate, A Social Interactional Approach to Child Abuse: Risk, Prevention and Treatment.

Rosenman, Ray H., Health Consequences of Anger and Implications for Treatment.

Siegel, Judith M., The Measurement of Anger as a Multidimensional Construct.

Spielberger, Charles D., Johnson, Ernest H. Russell, Stephen F., Crane, Rosario J., Jacobs, Gerard A., and Worden, Timothy J., The Experience and Expression of Anger: Construction and Validation of an Anger Expression Scale.

Williams, Jr., Redford B., Barefoot, John C., and Shekelle, Richard B., The Health Consequences of Hostility.

Cottington, Eric M., Matthews, Karen A., Talbott, Evelyn, and Kuller, Lewis H., Occupational Stress, Suppressed Anger and Hypertension, *Psychosomatic Medicine*, Vol. 48, No. 3/4. 1986.

Deffenbacher, Jerry L., Demm, P.M. and Brandon, Allen D., High General Anger: Correlates and Treatment. *Beh. Res. Ther.*, Vol. 24 #4, 481-489, 1986.

Dimsdale, Joel E., Pierce, Chester, Schoenfeld, David, Brown, Anne, Zusman, Randall, and Graham, Robert. Suppressed Anger and Blood Pressure: The Effects of Race, Sex, Social Class, Obesity and Age. *Psychosomatic Medicine*, Vol. 49, No. 6, 1986.

Ellis, Albert, *How to Live with and without Anger*, New York: Reader's Digest Press, 1977.

_____, *A Guide to Rational Living*. North Hollywood, Calif.: Wilshire Books, 1961.

BIBLIOGRAPHY

Hassebrauck, Manfred, Ragings of Distress as a Function of Degree and Kind of Inequity, *The Journal of Social Psychology*, 126 (2), 268-270, 1986.

Hazaleus, Susan L. and Deffenbacher, Jerry L., Relaxation and Cognitive Treatment of Anger. *Journal of Consulting and Clinical Psychology*, Vol. 54, No. 2, 222-226, 1986.

Julius, Mara, Harburg, Ernest, Cottington, Eric M. and Johnson, Ernest H., Anger-coping Types, Blood Pressure, and All-cause Mortality: A follow-up in Tecumseh, Michigan (1971-1983). *American Journal of Epidemiology*. The John Hopkins University School of Hygiene and Public Health. 1986.

Kiley, Dan, *Wendy Dilemma*. New York, Prentice Hall Press, 1989.

Leaf, Russell C., Gross, Paget Hope, Todres, Amy K., Marcus, Susan, and Bradford, Barry. Placebo-like Effects of Education about Rational-Emotive Therapy, *Psychological Reports*, 58, 351-370, 1986.

Lerner, Harriett Goldhor, *The Dance of Anger*. New York: Harper and Row, 1985.

McKay, Matthew, Rogers, Peter D., McKay, Judith, *When Anger Hurts*. Oakland, Calif.: New Harbinger Publications, Inc. 1989.

Miller, Annetta, Springer, Karen, Gordon, Jeanne, Murr, Andrew, Cohn, Bob, Drew, Lisa, and Barrett, Todd. Stress on the Job, *Newsweek*, 40-48, April 25, 1988.

Nelson, Jane, *Positive Discipline*, Fair Oaks, Calif. Sunrise Press, 1981.

Norwood, Robin, *Women Who Love Too Much*, New York. Pocket Books, a Division of Simon and Schuster. 1986.

BIBLIOGRAPHY

Oliver, Carol H. and Schneider, Eric, Communication Awareness: Rx for Angry Patients, *American Pharmacy*, Vol. NS26, No. 3, 93-94, March 1986-249.

Rubin, Theodore I., *The Angry Book*, New York: McMillan Publishing Co. 1969.

Schneider, Robert H., Egan, Brent M., Johnson, Ernest H., Drobny, Herman, and Herman, and Julius, Stevo, Anger and Anxiety in Borderline Hypertension. New York, *Psychomatic Medicine*, Vol. 48, No. 3/4 (March/April) 1986.

Siegel, Judith M., The Multidimensional Anger Inventory. *Journal of Personality and Social Psychology*, Vol. 51, No. 1, 191-200. 1986.

Sonkin, Daniel Jay and Durphy, Michael, *Learning to Live Without Violence*. San Francisco: Volcano Publishing Co. 1985.

Tavris, Carol. *Anger, the Misunderstood Emotion*, New York: Simon and Schuster, 1982.

Weisinger, Hendrie. *Dr. Weisinger's Anger Work Out Book*, New York: Quill, 1985.

Index

ORDER FORM   The Bookery Publishing Co.

8193 Riata Dr., Redding, CA 96002 • (916) 365-8068 or 365-8082
Order by phone or mail. Full refund if not satisfied.

Please send me the following books:

_____ copies of **SHAKE THE ANGER HABIT!** $ _____
(Doty/Rooney) — $11.95 — ISBN 0-930822-10-2
... **revised edition** includes "The Angry Pleasers"...

_____ copies of **THE ANGER PUZZLE** $ _____
(Doty/Rooney) — $8.95 — ISBN 0-930822-07-2
... you don't need to push others away with your anger,
a beginner's guide ...

_____ copies of **BREAK THE ANGER TRAP** $ _____
(Doty) — $8.95 — ISBN 0-930822-06-4
... includes worksheets for processing your own anger

_____ copies of **MARRIAGE INSURANCE** $ _____
(Doty) — $8.95 — ISBN 0-930822-01-3
... a series of communication exercises for two people
to use together

_____ copies of $ _____
PUBLISH YOUR OWN HANDBOUND BOOKS
(Doty) — $12.95 — ISBN 0-930822-02-1
... for writers who don't mind using copy-machine printing
and handbinding in order to begin the fun of publishing...
a bookbinding kit is tucked under the dust jacket.

★★NEW★★
_____ Audio Cassette(s) **SHAKE THE ANGER HABIT!** $ _____
(the essentials, 1 hr.) — $10.95 — ISBN 0-930822-11-0
... for individuals, personnel managers, program coordinators,
or ANYONE interested in anger... (includes diagrams and
discussion outline)

_____ Audio Cassette(s) **SHAKE THE ANGER HABIT!** $ _____
(entire book) — $24.95 — ISBN 0-930822-12-9
(includes diagrams and discussion outline)

	Subtotal:	$ _____
Less Discount (20% discount for 3 or more items):		$ _____
	Subtotal:	$ _____
Californians: please add 6.25% tax:		$ _____
Flat rate for shipping any number of items:		$ __2.00__
	TOTAL ENCLOSED:	$ _____

☐ Check here if you would like to be on a mailing list to receive notice about
anger seminars in your area. Or phone Rebecca Meredith (916) 365-8068 or
365-8082.

Ship books to: _____

_____

_____

_____

_____

ORDER FORM
The Bookery Publishing Co.

8193 Riata Dr., Redding, CA 96002 • (916) 365-8068 or 365-8082
Order by phone or mail. Full refund if not satisfied.

Please send me the following books:

_____ copies of **SHAKE THE ANGER HABIT!** $ _____
(Doty/Rooney) — $11.95 — ISBN 0-930822-10-2
... **revised edition** includes "The Angry Pleasers"...

_____ copies of **THE ANGER PUZZLE** $ _____
(Doty/Rooney) — $8.95 — ISBN 0-930822-07-2
... you don't need to push others away with your anger,
a beginner's guide ...

_____ copies of **BREAK THE ANGER TRAP** $ _____
(Doty) — $8.95 — ISBN 0-930822-06-4
... includes worksheets for processing your own anger

_____ copies of **MARRIAGE INSURANCE** $ _____
(Doty) — $8.95 — ISBN 0-930822-01-3
... a series of communication exercises for two people
to use together

_____ copies of $ _____
PUBLISH YOUR OWN HANDBOUND BOOKS
(Doty) — $12.95 — ISBN 0-930822-02-1
... for writers who don't mind using copy-machine printing
and handbinding in order to begin the fun of publishing...
a bookbinding kit is tucked under the dust jacket.

★★NEW★★

_____ Audio Cassette(s) **SHAKE THE ANGER HABIT!** $ _____
(the essentials, 1 hr.) — $10.95 — ISBN 0-930822-11-0
... for individuals, personnel managers, program coordinators,
or ANYONE interested in anger... (includes diagrams and
discussion outline)

_____ Audio Cassette(s) **SHAKE THE ANGER HABIT!** $ _____
(entire book) — $24.95 — ISBN 0-930822-12-9
(includes diagrams and discussion outline)

Subtotal:	$ _____
Less Discount (20% discount for 3 or more items):	$ _____
Subtotal:	$ _____
Californians: please add 6.25% tax:	$ _____
Flat rate for shipping any number of items:	$ __2.00__
TOTAL ENCLOSED:	$ _____

☐ Check here if you would like to be on a mailing list to receive notice about
anger seminars in your area. Or phone Rebecca Meredith (916) 365-8068 or
365-8082.

Ship books to: _____